VITAMINS & MINERALS

AN ILLUSTRATED GUIDE

VITAMINS & MINERALS

AN ILLUSTRATED GUIDE

KAREN SULLIVAN

Shaftesbury, Dorset • Boston, Massachusetts • Melbourne, Victoria

© Element Books Limited 1998

First published in Great Britain in 1998 by
ELEMENT BOOKS LIMITED
Shaftesbury, Dorset, SP7 8BP

Published in the USA in 1998 by
ELEMENT BOOKS INC
160 North Washington Street, Boston MA 02114

Published in Australia in 1998 by
ELEMENT BOOKS
and distributed by Penguin Australia Ltd
487 Maroondah Highway, Ringwood, Victoria 3134

NOTE FROM THE PUBLISHER
*Any information given in this book is not intended to be taken
as a replacement for medical advice. Any person with a condition
requiring medical attention should consult a qualified
practitioner or therapist.*

Designed and created with
The Bridgewater Book Company Limited

ELEMENT BOOKS LIMITED
Creative Director: ED DAY
Managing Editor: MIRANDA SPICER
Senior Commissioning Editor: CARO NESS
Editor: KATIE WORRALL
Production Manager: SUSAN SUTTERBY

THE BRIDGEWATER BOOK COMPANY
Art Director: KEVIN KNIGHT
Designer: JANE LANAWAY
Managing Editor: ANNE TOWNLEY
Editor: CAROLINE EARLE
Picture Research: LYNDA MARSHALL

Printed and bound in Great Britain
by Butler and Tanner, Frome

Library of Congress Cataloging in Publication
data available

British Library Cataloging in Publication
data available

ISBN 1–86204–295–0

Picture credits
*The publisher would like to thank
the following for the use of pictures:*
AKG, London: 81
Bridgeman Art Library: 65c (British Museum, London)
Harry Smith Collection: 81b
Hulton-Deutsch Collection/Corbis Images: 8r
Image Bank: 11b, 16r, 17r, 18, 41l, 44l, 60b, 60r, 67, 68l, 80b, 86t, 100t, 100l,
103b, 104t, 104b, 109b, 112t, 123b, 128t
Images Colour Library: 53, 92c
Robert Harding Library: 56l
Science Photo Library: 43b, 47b, 55b, 64r, 69l, 72b, 75t, 79b, 82l, 83bl, 117t,
120b, 135t, 136t
Stock Market: 2, 16l, 27r, 39r, 46c, 112t

Acknowledgments
Special thanks to
Lily Adams, Tom Aitken, Cristina Fagarazzi, Jessie Fuller,
Geoffrey Gardeney, Joseph Harding, R. Harding,
N. Hobby, H. Jordan, Jeanne Lewington, J. Phillips, S. Sains,
Anna Spyropoulos, Julie Spyropoulos, Julie Whitaker, Deborah Wright,
Emily Wright, Victoria Wright
for help with photography.

Contents

PREFACE   6

HOW TO USE THIS BOOK   7

A HISTORY OF
NUTRITIONAL THERAPY   8

THE ROLE OF
NUTRITIONAL THERAPY   10

EATING WELL AND USING
SUPPLEMENTS   12

VISITING A PROFESSIONAL   24

THE LISTINGS   28

HOW TO USE THIS SECTION   29

VITAMINS   30

MINERALS AND TRACE ELEMENTS   46

OTHER HELPFUL SUPPLEMENTS   66

SUPPLEMENTS FOR
OVERALL GOOD HEALTH   86

SELF-HELP FOR ILLNESSES   114

FURTHER READING   140

USEFUL ADDRESSES   141

INDEX   142

Preface

THE IMPORTANCE OF DIET *in preventive medicine and treatment is becoming increasingly acknowledged, and diet is probably the area in which we can make the greatest impact on general health and vitality, the prevention of disease, and the treatment of illnesses.*

Awareness of vitamins, minerals, and trace elements is relatively new. Until recently, nutrition played a very small role in the conventional treatment of health problems.

ABOVE *Many people now supplement their diet with vitamins, minerals, and other nutritional elements.*

Today, the stresses of daily living and the assault on our bodies by environmental pollutants, among other things, have led to an extraordinary array of health problems, which has forced an investigation into the relationship between health and the elements of nutrition. Part of the reason for this investigation is the fact that many people are now accepting more responsibility for their own health and paying more attention to diet, exercise, and emotions. They are slowly but surely making the switch to a "new" set of medicinal substances – herbs and nutrients that work with the body to keep it well. Unlike some conventional drugs, which may relieve symptoms but do nothing to address the root cause of illness, natural substances, such as vitamins, minerals, and the other essential nutrients, work quite differently.

BELOW *We are now more aware of the importance of a well-balanced healthy diet that includes plenty of fruit.*

ABOVE *Exercise plays an important role in maintaining a fit and healthy body.*

How to Use This Book

This book comprises three principal sections, starting with an outline of the history and role of nutritional therapy. The Listings, cataloging the available range of nutritional supplements, make up the main part of the book. Final chapters explain how to treat illnesses and maintain good health.

BELOW **Early chapters highlight the importance of nutrition and supplements in maintaining health.**

Clear text explains the role that vitamin or mineral deficiency can play in ill-health, and highlights the ways in which we are all at risk.

In the Listings, each of the principal supplements is described, together with its role in the body. A dosage panel suggests the quantities in which it should be taken.

BELOW **The Listings give full details of all the major supplements – vitamins, minerals, and others.**

An illustrated box lists the effects of particular deficiencies, and the possible dietary or physical causes are explained.

BELOW **Final chapters explain the relevance of particular diets and supplements in fulfilling your specific health needs.**

A box for each illness outlines its main causes, the supplements that should be taken to improve the condition, and the doses in which they should be used.

Information boxes detail the properties, symptoms of a deficiency, and the sources of the substance; Special Notes point out any potential side effects.

Particular illnesses are grouped according to the body system that they affect, and their symptoms are described.

A History of Nutritional Therapy

"LET FOOD BE YOUR MEDICINE and medicine be your food," wrote Hippocrates in the fifth century B.C.E., and, indeed, from the very earliest days of civilization, nutrition has formed the backbone of healthcare. Well before he was writing, obtaining and eating food consumed a vast amount of time and energy, and food and herbs were our first medicine, used to treat a large number of conditions. It has always been clear, to one degree or another, that food has a medicinal effect, and that a varied diet, rich in natural ingredients, is a prerequisite for good health. From the earliest times, diet became a fundamental part of many therapies, and an integral element of most.

ABOVE *Hippocrates (c. 469–399 B.C.E.) recognized the importance of a nutritious diet in healthcare.*

NATUROPATHY

In the late 19th century, naturopaths drew attention to the use of food and its nutritional elements as medicine, a concept that was not new, but which had not been acknowledged as a therapy in its own right until that time. Naturopaths used nutrition and fasting to cleanse the body, and to encourage its ability to heal itself. With the development of bio-chemistry, knowledge about food, its makeup, and the effects that it has on our body became greater, and the first nutritional specialists undertook to treat specific ailments and symptoms with the components of food.

By the middle of the 20th century, scientists had put together a profile of proteins, carbohydrates, and fats, as well as vitamins and minerals, that were essential to life and to health. More than 40 nutrients were uncovered, including 13 vitamins. It was discovered that minerals were needed for body functions, and understanding of the body and its biochemistry grew. In the 1960s, the controversial fields of orthomolecular psychiatry and orthomolecular medicine were defined, and physicians began to treat patients with special diets and supplements, prescribed according to individual symptoms, problems, and needs. While conventional medical physicians still discussed nutrition in terms of basic food groups (only three days of medical school is turned over to the subject), orthomolecular nutritionists were

LEFT *Laboratory work from the 1950s onward has extended our understanding of the nutritional qualities of food.*

prescribing vitamins in megadoses. Physicians used biochemicals to correct nutritional deficiencies they saw as factors in a huge range of physical and mental diseases.

From that time the field spread from being mainly physician-led dietary therapy, also called clinical nutrition, into a more profound theory of health based on treating the patient as a whole (holistic health), and looking for deficiencies that may be causing illness, which are specific to each individual.

THE WESTERN DIET

While this research into diet was on-going, however, the average Western diet was on a downward spiral. Modern methods of farming and production, as well as the huge boom in convenience foods, meant that most of us were getting fewer, rather than more, nutrients from our food, and suffering the often long-term consequences of deficiency (see pp. 16–17). Furthermore, an overdependence upon drugs, and physicians, for healthcare, caused most of us to put the responsibility for our health into the hands of others, which resulted in a lack of objectivity about diet and health, and a loss of intuition about our own bodies.

When we suffer an ailment or an illness, chronic or severe, we trot along to the physician, never stopping to analyze the reasons why such illnesses might be occurring. Understanding our own bodies is the fundamental basis of both preventive healthcare and treatment, and by ignoring our body's messages, we are unable to

LASAGNE
RATATOUILLE
PIZZA

ABOVE *An overreliance on convenience foods in our daily diet can result in nutritional deficiency.*

reason when and why we feel good, and when and why we don't. Diet has an enormous impact on our physical and mental health, and the food we eat has both therapeutic and preventive benefits. Only now are we beginning to correlate the fact that our health problems may be caused by the foods we are, or are not, eating.

BELOW *Lemons and limes are rich in vitamin C. They were given to sailors in the 18th century to prevent scurvy.*

LIMES

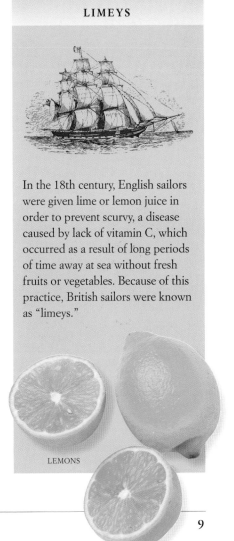

LIMEYS

In the 18th century, English sailors were given lime or lemon juice in order to prevent scurvy, a disease caused by lack of vitamin C, which occurred as a result of long periods of time away at sea without fresh fruits or vegetables. Because of this practice, British sailors were known as "limeys."

LEMONS

9

The Role of Nutritional Therapy

WE DON'T ALWAYS EAT well, despite the choice of food we have. Yet good food – because of its nutrient content – is crucial to our well-being. Nutritional therapy addresses the causes of much ill-health by examining what we eat. As a therapy it works by both prescription and elimination: it prescribes nutrients to treat specific illnesses, and it helps to identify foods that may trigger allergic responses.

About fifteen vitamins, eighteen minerals, and eight to ten amino acids have been isolated as being essential for normal body functions. These nutrients are synergistic, which means that they work together to keep the body functioning at optimum level. When one or more nutrients is in short supply, the body cannot function properly, and symptoms – both mental and physical – occur. For example, a lack of vitamin C – vital for the immune system – results in poor resistance to infection, bleeding gums, and slow wound

WHOLE-WHEAT BREAD

CHEESE

MILK

WHEAT

ABOVE *Certain foods, such as wheat and dairy products, may cause allergic reactions in some people.*

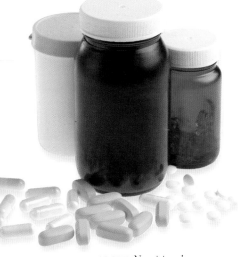

ABOVE *Nutritional therapists often prescribe dietary supplements in the form of tablets.*

healing. Nutrients are the chemical components of food and are essential to life, and to health. The therapeutic prescription of nutrients – prescribing nutrients to treat illness – is known as nutritional therapy, and practitioners specializing in it are nutritional therapists. Nutrients prescribed in this way are called dietary or food supplements, and they come in the form of tablets, capsules, powders, or liquids. On certain occasions, nutrients may be injected directly into the body for greater effect.

Nutritional therapy has been a complementary therapy in its own right for only a short period of time, largely because our knowledge of nutrition is still in its infancy. However, nutrition has formed the backbone of many other complementary therapies, some of which have been practiced for thousands of years. Most good therapists in any complementary discipline will ask you about your diet and lifestyle, and offer advice on nutrition to insure that your body is working at optimum level.

Nutritional therapy involves prescribing special diets to alleviate specific ailments. Food allergies or intolerances may contribute to ill-health. Elimination diets that advocate avoiding certain suspect substances, often wheat and dairy produce, can be an important part of treatment. But in such cases the therapist must determine the underlying imbalance that leads to the intolerance. In other words, the intolerance can be a symptom of a greater problem such as digestive disease or irritated mucous membranes that is caused by following a poor diet.

OVERFED AND UNDERNOURISHED

The typical diet in the Western "civilized" world provides far from adequate nutrition. In fact, it does the opposite, contributing not only to ill-health but to obesity, heart disease, cancer, digestive disorders, premature aging, and in many cases death. The Western world is overfed and undernourished, and although food is plentiful, it is often food devoid of any nutritional value.

BELOW *Many of the foods we eat are nutritionally poor, and should only be eaten as an occasional treat.*

SUPPLEMENTING A DIET

Every one of us will benefit from an improved diet and prudent use of supplements according to our individual needs. Human bodies were not designed to cope with modern-day stresses, or the huge number of physical demands placed upon them, largely in the form of dietary and environmental toxins. We now have the power to influence not only our own health but also that of our families and future generations. Armed with that knowledge, we can enjoy an enhanced quality of life and experience optimum health and well-being, living longer and better than ever before.

Supplements are preparations of vitamins, minerals, amino acids, essential fatty acids (E.F.A.s), enzymes, fiber, and other factors that have a use or necessary physiological function in the body. They are either found in food or synthesized within the body, when food is ingested. Supplements may be chemically synthesized, or they may be natural extracts. Examples of supplements include concentrated plant or animal source preparations, such as fish oils, yeast, probiotics, algae, and plant or herb extracts. Supplements are used either to provide nutrition or for their therapeutic properties.

SEAWEED

ABOVE *The effects of modern-day stress mean that obtaining the correct balance of nutrients is vital if we want to work hard and play hard.*

Eating Well and Using Supplements

THE FIRST STEP *to a healthy diet is to develop good shopping habits. The fresher your food, and the closer to its natural state (a potato, rather than chips, for example), the better it is for you. The next steps are good habits of storage and of preparation. Unfortunately, the way in which the majority of our food is now produced may mean that even a healthy diet can be deficient in nutrients, and supplements may be advisable.*

A HEALTHY DIET

Each individual body has different requirements, based partly on the type of metabolism inherited, and on lifestyle and eating habits. Some people appear to be able to eat whatever they want and remain in good health. Others have defined weaknesses, and what would be considered a balanced diet for one, may not be appropriate for the individual needs of another.

A healthy diet is one in which the food you eat contains all the nutrients needed by the body for it to grow, heal, and undertake all of the processes necessary to life. It provides energy and allows you to function at your optimum level, free from disease and malaise. To insure you get maximum nutrients, choose fresh and unrefined foods from local sources where possible.

Ideally, vitamins and minerals can be found in all natural foods, but in reality, processing and other modern methods of food production and refining, as well as overindulgence in alcohol and caffeine-laden drinks, mean that there may be very little in our daily diets.

BELOW *A well-balanced diet consists of carbohydrates, fruits and vegetables, protein, and some fat.*

WHOLE-WHEAT BREAD

RED GRAPES

RED AND GREEN BELL PEPPERS

APPLE

BROCCOLI

SOYBEANS

RAISINS

WHITE GRAPES

HAZELNUTS

CHEESE

BANANA

ALMONDS

SPINACH

LIMA BEANS

PARSLEY

KIDNEY BEANS

ORANGE

DILL

LENTILS

BROWN RICE

DIETARY TIPS

Our diet should be made up of complex carbohydrates (five to nine portions per day), fruits and vegetables (four to nine portions), proteins (three to five portions), and fat (under 1oz./30g). A complex carbohydrate is a carbohydrate that is not refined or processed. A portion is a regular serving size: a couple of medium-size potatoes, for example. But eating the right foods doesn't necessarily mean that you are getting enough nutrients. Refining and processing foods takes out most of the nutritional value, and pesticides and other agents used in the growing process place extra demands on our bodies. Before our food even reaches the supermarket it may be nutritionally deficient. Take extra steps to preserve the nutritional content of your food:

• Eat the skins of vegetables whenever possible.

• Don't cut, wash, or soak fruits and vegetables until you are ready to eat them. Exposing their cut surfaces to air reduces many of their nutrients.

• Eat brown, unpolished rice, and wholegrains.

• Choose fresh fruit and vegetables first, but remember that nutritional value decreases with age. Frozen is a better option if you aren't going to eat the food immediately.

• Eat raw whenever possible; if cooking, use only a little water.

• If you do boil fruits or vegetables, use the water in your sauces.

• Eat organic food whenever possible. It may be a little more expensive, but you can be sure that the food you are eating has not been processed and has been grown without the use of pesticides and other chemicals.

BROCCOLI

BRUSSELS SPOUTS

CAULIFLOWER

CABBAGE

ABOVE *To retain nutrients, do not wash, soak, or cut vegetables or other foods until you are ready to cook and eat them.*

IS A HEALTHY DIET EXPENSIVE?

A good diet doesn't need to be expensive, and it is quite likely to be cheaper than a poor diet. For example, there is no need to eat expensive cuts of meat every day (vegetable proteins, such as lentils and tofu, are cheap in comparison), and fresh foods are always much cheaper than ready-prepared, refined products. Your main problem may be finding the time to buy fresh food several times a week, then to cook and eat properly, but that can be overcome with a little organization. Having a freezer helps. Take time to make a big, fresh vegetable stew or soup, with plenty of pulses, and freeze it in small quantities as soon as it is prepared to give you a nutritious meal at hand when time is tight. Rice and pulses can also be prepared and cooked in large batches and frozen.

BELOW *Preparing nutritional foods for your freezer will insure that you have a ready supply of healthy meals.*

What We Need from Food

THERE ARE MANY ELEMENTS *in food. Proteins, carbohydrates, fats, and fiber are the most important, but equally necessary is the fine-tuning provided by vitamins and minerals. Wholefoods – foods that are unrefined and unprocessed – supply nutrients in their natural state, and are therefore likely to be much better for us. Manufacturing processes destroy nutrients and upset the natural balance of foods. It is worthwhile understanding what is in the food you eat, and the best forms in which to eat it.*

Five different food groups make up a healthy diet: fats, carbohydrates, proteins, minerals, and vitamins. You also need water, which is found in most foods and makes up a large proportion of our body. Proteins should make up about 15 percent of the diet, carbohydrates 60 percent or more, and fats a maximum of 25 to 30 percent. Vitamins and minerals are found within each of these groups, and a balanced diet should have all or most represented in adequate levels. In the body, proteins, carbohydrates, and fats combine with other substances to yield energy and build bones and tissue. These chemical reactions are accelerated by specific vitamins and take place all over the body. The vitamins that we need are divided into two categories – water-soluble vitamins (the B vitamins and vitamin C) and fat-soluble vitamins (A, D, E, and K).

The water-soluble vitamins are absorbed by the intestine and carried in the bloodstream to the tissues where they will be put into use. Water-soluble vitamins are not stored in the body and must be taken daily to prevent deficiency. They serve very many diverse functions in the body.

Fat-soluble vitamins have specialized functions. The intestine absorbs them, and the lymphatic system carries them to the different parts of the body. They are involved in maintaining the structure of cell membranes. Excessive intake of fat-soluble vitamins, particularly vitamins A and D, can lead to toxic levels in the body.

Without the 18 known minerals required for the maintenance of our bodies, vitamins cannot be assimilated effectively.

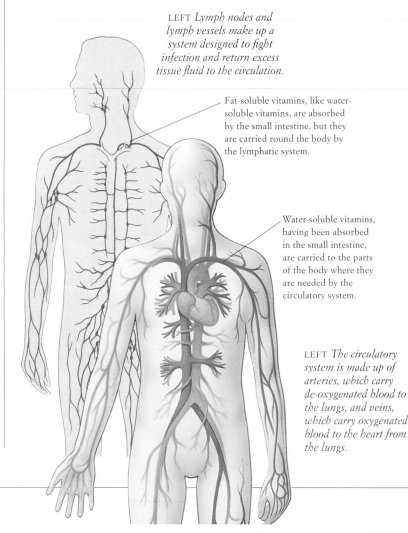

LEFT *Lymph nodes and lymph vessels make up a system designed to fight infection and return excess tissue fluid to the circulation.*

Fat-soluble vitamins, like water-soluble vitamins, are absorbed by the small intestine, but they are carried round the body by the lymphatic system.

Water-soluble vitamins, having been absorbed in the small intestine, are carried to the parts of the body where they are needed by the circulatory system.

LEFT *The circulatory system is made up of arteries, which carry de-oxygenated blood to the lungs, and veins, which carry oxygenated blood to the heart from the lungs.*

CHOOSING FRESH AND WHOLESOME FOODS

The Western diet is in general high in cholesterol and fats (especially unhealthy saturated fats), low in dietary fiber, and high in refined sugars and animal products. People who eat diets that are low in fat and cholesterol, and high in dietary fiber, fruits, and vegetables are thinner, healthier, and have much more energy. Ailments such as aches and pains, headaches, diabetes, immune deficiencies, skin problems, and digestive disorders can all be linked to a nutritionally poor diet, and symptoms have disappeared in many people who decide to change their eating habits and follow a nutritionally sound diet.

RED BELL PEPPER

CURLY KALE

POTATOES

BABY CORN

GREEN BELL PEPPER

SNOW PEAS

PARSLEY

BROCCOLI

BLACK GRAPES

BANANA

ORANGE

PEAR

WHITE GRAPES

RICE

RED LENTILS

KIDNEY BEANS

SPECIAL DIETS

A number of diets are based around special needs; for instance, sufferers of heart disease should adopt low-fat and low-salt diets. Other special diets treat illness through fasting and eating raw food to cleanse the system. As a general rule, however, diets should be varied, with as few restrictions as possible.

Fresh fruits, vegetables, and salads should appear in your daily diet, and fresh meat and fish should be used in place of packaged or frozen foods. Many of the processes used to preserve food, such as freezing and canning, can result in a loss of nutrients. Wherever possible, try to choose foods that are fresh and local, since long storage or periods of traveling can cause nutrients to be lost. Read the labels of foods carefully, avoiding any products that contain flavorings, preservatives, and colorings, many of which can be toxic.

ABOVE *Unrefined foods have the benefits of being more nutritious and helping the digestive process.*

WHOLEFOODS

A good diet is based around wholefoods, which means unrefined foods. Parts of the food are removed during the refining process and in this way vital nutrients and natural fiber are lost. The result is a product with a reduced nutritional value, and one that is less easily digested, since natural fiber aids the process of elimination and digestion. Organically produced foods should be eaten whenever possible, although they are, unfortunately, generally more expensive than their nonorganic equivalent.

LEFT *Eat organically whenever possible. Organic food has far more nutritional value.*

Signs of Deficiency

VITAMIN OR MINERAL DEFICIENCIES *do not always manifest themselves as major health problems, since most of us are not severely deficient in any single nutrient. However, marginal deficiencies are very common, and are likely to be responsible for many minor overlooked symptoms, such as a predisposition to headaches, difficulty sleeping, or skin complaints. Minor problems, left untreated, can become more serious, which is why it is important to deal with any nutritional imbalances or small deficiencies as soon as possible.*

Few people have signs of a serious vitamin or mineral deficiency, such as scurvy or pellagra, but it is now widely accepted that many people have slight shortages of minerals or vitamins, called "subclinical deficiencies," which show up as mild ill-health, fatigue, susceptibility to infections, and other niggling health problems, such as headaches, insomnia, irritability, and digestive problems. Certain people are quite likely to eat a less than balanced diet, including those who can't afford or don't have time to buy fresh fruit

ABOVE *If juggling a hectic work and domestic life means relying on convenience foods, you may not be getting all of the nutrients you need.*

and vegetables, or people who rely on refined or convenience foods. Women are often too busy to look after their own nutritional needs, and studies show that 20 percent of women of childbearing age are nutritionally deficient. Women who have had a baby recently, or who are breast-feeding, may be a little short of a variety of nutrients, since their bodies are helping to nourish the baby's growth.

While the initial symptoms of subclinical nutritional deficiencies may be only minor, damage and disturbance to metabolic functions are potentially very dangerous. For example, a lack of antioxidant nutrients can cause an increased level of highly toxic intermediates, such as acetaldehyde, which are produced by the liver in the course of detoxification and which would otherwise be canceled out by the

LEFT *It is important to take account of the additional nutritional demands which breast-feeding creates.*

antioxidants. The accumulation of such substances has been linked with diseases such as Parkinson's disease and motor neurone disease. However, because such serious diseases take a long time to develop, no connection with nutritional deficiencies is currently accepted by the conventional medical establishment.

Certain groups of the population are particularly vulnerable to nutritional deficiencies, including pregnant or lactating women, those on weight-loss diets, children, adolescents, and the elderly.

CAUSES OF DEFICIENCY

Nutritional deficiency may be caused by any of the following:

- Inadequate intake
- Inadequate digestion
- Inadequate absorption
- Inadequate assimilation
- Increased needs
- Increased losses

RIGHT *Making sure children eat a balanced diet is especially important, as they are particularly vulnerable to nutritional deficiencies.*

POSSIBLE DEFICIENCY SYMPTOMS

Your body will make clear when even small deficiencies are present. What follows is a list of symptoms which may result from a shortfall of particular nutrients:

SYMPTOM	DEFICIENCY
Hair problems	vitamins B12, B6; selenium
Eye problems	vitamins A, C
Nervousness	B6, B12, B3, B5, magnesium, vitamin C
Infections	vitamins A, B-complex, C; biotin, calcium, potassium, zinc
Fatigue	zinc, iron, vitamins A, B, C, D
Constipation	B-complex, vitamin C
Diarrhea	vitamins A, niacin (B3), B12, K
Muscle cramps	vitamins B1 and D, biotin, sodium, magnesium, calcium
Skin problems	vitamins A, B-complex; biotin, copper

TESTING

If you want to know whether or not you need to supplement, it is always best to contact a nutritionist, or nutritional therapist, who will be able to undertake a variety of tests to pinpoint your exact needs. Dozens of laboratory tests are available to nutritional therapists in order for them to make their diagnoses, and they measure everything from sugar intolerance and blood levels of vitamins and minerals, to thyroid function and levels of insulin. Hair analysis can evaluate levels of trace minerals and reveal dietary habits, and the intake and level of toxins can be uncovered.

BELOW *Laboratory tests help to determine which supplements are necessary for a particular person.*

LEFT *Vitamin and mineral deficiencies show up in the body in a variety of ailments and diseases.*

Toxic Overload

THE FOOD THAT WE EAT *is rarely pure. It may have been sprayed, injected, grown in chemically rich soil, or fed on unsuitable food. Even worse, perhaps, some of our food is now genetically modified and the long-term effects of these procedures on our health are yet to be discovered. One of the main jobs of our body is to convert toxins into safe substances – but modern living is taking its toll. Our systems are overloaded to previously unimagined levels, putting our bodies under enormous pressure to "detoxify." The good news is that there are nutrients that can help.*

ABOVE *Much of the plant food that we eat has been sprayed with harmful pesticides and insecticides.*

Most of the food that we buy has been preserved, sprayed with chemicals, injected, or grown in chemically rich soil. Plant food is treated with pesticides and insecticides, and animals are pumped full of antibiotics and growth hormones.

Pollution in growing areas adds further chemicals to the food that we eat. As a result, much of our food, rather than offering nutrients, adds further to our toxic overload, and becomes yet another stress on our bodies.

Toxic overload is a dangerous condition, and it is believed to be the root of many of our health problems today. One of the body's most important functions is to convert products and toxins into soluble, safe substances that can be eliminated from the body through the bladder or the intestines. The liver is extremely important in this process, which is called detoxification. People who have been exposed to large numbers of toxins, including chemicals in foodstuff and drugs, will have increased requirements for most vitamins and minerals.

ALL ABOUT ANTIOXIDANTS

Antioxidants are compounds that inhibit chemical reactions with oxygen in the body. Oxidation reactions may involve highly reactive molecules called free radicals; metals, such as copper, often catalyze reactions with oxygen. Among these reactions are those that cause cell damage in the body. Antioxidants inhibit these changes by reacting with the free radicals before they can cause any damage (free radical scavenging) or by reacting with the metals. Naturally occurring antioxidants may also work by interacting directly with oxygen.

Nutrients called antioxidants – vitamins C, E, and beta-carotene, and the minerals zinc and selenium, among others – are now known to have an antiaging effect. Contained in fruits, nuts, and most vegetables, antioxidants are the body's defense against free radicals, which cause all types of cellular damage in the body. Free radicals are implicated in the initiation of cancer, heart disease, and even aging itself – so much so that many experts believe that the aging process is actually produced by the constant, tiny degenerative effects that are caused by free radicals as they oxidize various cells over time.

Antioxidants provide the body with a natural defense against free radicals, which is why it is now recommended that you eat foods that are rich in these nutrients. Even a good diet may not be rich in antioxidants, so it is usually suggested that you take a good antioxidant supplement each day. Many trials have shown that additional antioxidant vitamins – such as 2,000mg of C and 400mg of E daily – can significantly reduce the number of heart attacks, strokes, and

BELOW *Nuts, fresh fruits, and vegetables are a good antioxidant source.*

CARROTS

MANGO

BROCCOLI

BRAZIL NUTS

cataracts. Take care if you are on "blood-thining" drugs. Many flavonoids (*see p. 85*) also have antioxidant action, and the herb ginkgo biloba (*see p.80*) is a good source of antioxidant flavonoids, which are also known as proanthocyanidins.

RIGHT *Many experts believe that aging is caused by the degenerative effects of free radicals.*

ANTIOXIDANTS REDUCE THE INCIDENCE OF CATARACTS

ANTIOXIDANTS HELP THE AGING PROCESS TO SLOW DOWN

TAKE VITAMIN E TO HELP PREVENT HEART DISEASE BUT SEEK ADVICE IF YOU ARE ON "BLOOD-THINING" DRUGS

The skins of black cherries, blueberries, and blackberries also contain proanthocyanidins. Extracts of bilberry contain flavonoids known as anthocyanosides, which have a very powerful antioxidant activity, some say even more than vitamins C and E. Other antioxidants include the flavonoid quercetin, the enzymes methione reductase and catalase, a substance found in the liver known as lipoic acid, and the substance coenzyme Q10.

ABOVE *Blueberries are a source of particularly powerful antioxidants.*

How to take Supplements

WE CANNOT ALWAYS *be sure of getting all the nutrients we need from food, and supplements are designed to compensate for any shortfalls. Now available in a variety of forms, supplements can be taken in small, regular amounts as a form of health insurance or to treat minor health problems. Nutritional therapists, on the other hand, may prescribe larger doses to treat specific complaints.*

Two principal types of multivitamin preparations are available both to the public and to the medical profession: supplemental, or pro-phylactic, and therapeutic.

Supplemental vitamins often contain a range of one-half to one-and-a-half times the R.D.A. requirements except for vitamin D, which should not exceed 400 international units (iu), and vitamin A, which should not exceed 1,000 retinol equivalents. These multi-vitamin preparations are designed to help prevent disease and to supplement the diet in cases of unusual stress.

Therapeutic multivitamin prep-arations are prescribed by physicians only for deficiency states and for the nutritional support of severe pathological conditions.

WHEN TO TAKE SUPPLEMENTS

The best time to take supplements is usually after meals: absorption of the supplement is best when the body has bulky food to work on. Time-release formulas, in particular, need to be taken with food because their nutrients are slowly released over a period of hours. If there is not enough food to slow their passage through the body, they can pass the sites where they are normally absorbed before they have had a chance to release their nutrients. The label on your supplements should advise you of the best time to take them.

Vitamins and minerals work most effectively when taken evenly throughout the day. The water-soluble vitamins, especially vitamins B-complex and C, are excreted rapidly from the body, and breaking the dose into three parts to take after meals will give you the best

chance of maintaining a high body level. If this is not convenient, then take half the amount after breakfast and half after dinner. Minerals are essential for the proper absorption of vitamins, so make sure that you take them together.

WHAT IS MEGADOSING?

Megadosing, or megavitamin therapy, is the therapeutic use of vitamins in exceptionally large doses. The term megavitamin therapy is often misapplied. It should not be used when only moderately large supplementation is applied, such as in the correction of marginal deficiency states. There is a great deal of scientific research into the value and safety of megavitamin therapy. Some vitamins and minerals are safe in large quantities and will not upset the balance of the body when taken in "megadoses," but you need a good understanding of how they work in the body before you attempt to take large doses to achieve health.

LEFT *Multivitamins are available in tablet form to supplement the diet and prevent disease.*

If you have to take all your supplements at once, take them after your biggest meal of the day, whether it is dinner, breakfast, or lunch – the idea being that they are better absorbed with a large meal than a small one.

Try to avoid taking any one vitamin supplement in excess since it will upset the balance of the other nutrients in the body. If you have to take 1,000mg of vitamin C, for example, break it up into three equal doses with your three main meals, unless it is a time-release version, in which case you may take it in one dose with your main meal.

RIGHT *Most supplements work best on a full stomach. Generally take them after your main meal of the day.*

WHEN TO TAKE SUPPLEMENTS

Vitamins A, D, E (fat-soluble)	Take regularly with food.
Iron	On an empty stomach (although it can cause nausea in some cases; take with food if you suffer any symptoms).
Calcium	High doses should be taken at night or between meals.
Zinc	Zinc should be taken with a meal; can cause nausea if taken with insufficient food.
Vitamin B-complex	First thing in the morning for maximum efficiency, although safe any time.
Vitamin C	Most effective taken with meals, and safest at this time if you have an acid-sensitive stomach. Best taken in the morning because it may increase energy levels.
Magnesium	Can promote sleepiness, so best taken at night.
Multivitamins, antioxidants, minerals	Any time is effective and safe – minerals (except those above) can be taken with fluid alone.
Time-release supplements	Take with the main meal of the day.

MEASUREMENTS

International Units, iu, are a measurement system for the activity of vitamins A, D, and E. Many products, particularly those in the higher dosage range, are still sold in International Units, because we have become accustomed to their system. Scientists no longer use International Units, and prefer to measure vitamins by weight.

1iu vitamin A = 0.3mcg (micrograms)
1iu vitamin D = 0.025mcg
1iu vitamin E = 0.7mcg, as d-alpha tocopherol

Other vitamins and minerals are measured by weight:

microgram	**mcg**
milligram (1,000mcg)	**mg**
gram (1,000mg)	**g**

How Supplements are Made

Most vitamins are extracted from natural sources. Others are synthesized (recreated in the laboratory by human hand). Synthetic vitamins may cause toxic reactions in certain susceptible individuals, but natural vitamins are usually safe. Natural vitamins are therefore preferable to their synthesized equivalents, but the synthesized versions are often cheaper.

Natural supplements will contain a complex of nutrients that work together. Whereas, vitamin C is isolated as ascorbic acid, and synthesized as ascorbic acid alone, natural vitamin C (extracted from rosehips, for example) will contain bioflavonoids and related C-compounds. This makes the ascorbic acid more effective, more easily assimilated, and less likely to cause toxic or allergic reactions. Synthesized vitamins do work, but experts say that they may work on a slightly lower level than natural versions.

Supplements come in various different forms, and some may be more appropriate than others. The easiest way to find out what is best for you is to experiment – a powder may be easier to take, particularly for children or older people. Some liquids and oils may cause a reaction in susceptible individuals; if that's the case for you, try another form.

RIGHT *Vitamin C, obtained naturally from rosehips, will contain bioflavonoids.*

All supplements have different quantities of the active ingredients. Check the quantity and the dosage recommended. This will be given as a percentage of the R.D.A. *(see p. 29)*. If you are in doubt, ask the store assistant to explain the label.

BELOW *Children and elderly people may find it easier to take their supplements in powder form.*

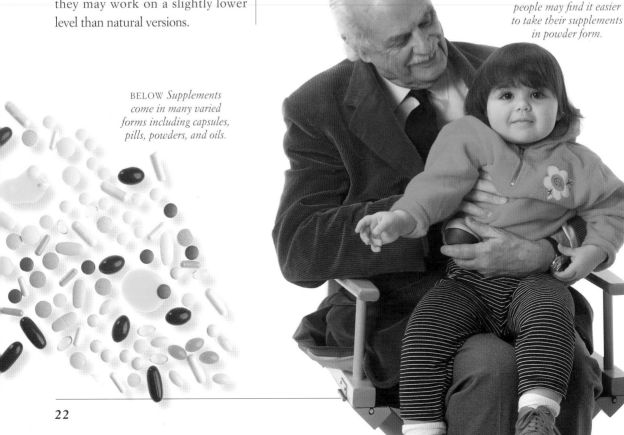

BELOW *Supplements come in many varied forms including capsules, pills, powders, and oils.*

THE DIFFERENT FORMS OF SUPPLEMENTS

Powders
Many vitamins and minerals come in this form – particularly vitamin C. It will provide you with extra potency, with no binders or additives (useful for people with allergies).

Capsules
These are convenient to take and easy to keep. Fat-soluble vitamins are normally taken in capsule form. A capsule may contain oil or powder; powders allow a higher potency.

Liquids
These are appropriate for people who have difficulty swallowing tablets or capsules. Many children's formulas come in liquid form for easy administration. Liquids can be mixed with food or drinks.

Tablets
Most vitamins and minerals come in tablet form and these are the most practical for many people because they can be easily stored and keep for a long time. Check the label to see what is added to your tablets in the form of binders or fillers, which are added to preserve or bulk out the active ingredient.

Chelation
Chelated is a term that will appear on mineral supplements, and it means combined with amino acids to make assimilation more efficient. It is always recommended that chelated products be used because they are three to five times more effective than nonchelated products.

OIL

Time-release
Time-release formulas are created by a process that allows them to be released into the body over an eight- to ten-hour period. These are particularly useful for water-soluble vitamins (see p.14), any excess of which is excreted within two or three hours of taking the supplement. Studies show that time-release formulas are most effective and provide stable blood levels during the day and night.

CAPSULES

WHAT IS IN YOUR SUPPLEMENTS

Most supplements contain extra ingredients either to preserve or bind the nutrients, or to act as a filler. Some people may be allergic to some of these "extras," and it is important to read the label to see what other ingredients might have been added.

Coatings
Vitamins are coated to protect the ingredients inside, and occasionally to mask a flavor or odor, or to make the tablet easier to swallow.

Flavorings
Flavors and sweeteners may be used in chewable tablets, and usually take the form of fructose (fruit sugar), malt dextrines, sorbitol, or maltose. Sugar is not usually used.

Lubricants
Tablets are lubricated to keep them from becoming adhered to the machines that punch them out. Calcium, stearate, and silica are commonly used.

Binders
Binders are the materials that hold together the ingredients of a tablet. Cellulose and ethyl cellulose are most often used, although acacia, a vegetable gum, or algin, a plant carbohydrate, may be used. Lecithin and sorbitol may also bind the ingredients in some products.

Fillers
Fillers are added to supplements to make them a practical size for taking. The most common filler is dicalcium phosphate, POWDER which is a good source of calcium and phosphate. Cellulose and sorbitol may also be used.

Colors
Many supplements are colored in order to make the product more appealing. Most good supplements are colored with natural sources, such as carotene. Keep all supplements away from children.

TABLETS

Visiting a Professional

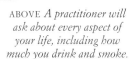

MINOR SYMPTOMS OF ILL-HEALTH *can safely be treated at home with careful supplementation, but to treat a specific illness, you need the advice of a registered practitioner. You will need to ask your physician for a referral to a nutritional practitioner unless your physician has specially trained in nutrition, and you may be advised to see to a nutritional therapist, a dietitian, or a clinical nutritionist.*

ABOVE *A practitioner will ask about every aspect of your life, including how much you drink and smoke.*

If you are looking for a general improvement in your health rather than wishing to address a particular ailment, you can probably treat yourself at home safely, without upsetting the fine balance of the body. However, if you wish to take supplements for a health condition, you are advised to see a registered practitioner, who can run a series of tests to ascertain any nutritional deficiencies and prescribe supplements that are required for your individual needs.

Your physician may recommend a dietician who works in his or her practice, or alternatively you may be referred to a clinical nutritionist, particularly if you are suffering from chronic health problems. Nutritional therapists work outside the conventional medical system, but may work with a physician or a group of other complementary practitioners. Qualified nutritional

LEFT *During your consultation, you will be asked about any medication that you take.*

therapists will be registered with their regulatory board and will be able to prove that they have undergone a rigorous and authorized course in nutrition.

A FULL CASE HISTORY WILL BE TAKEN

YOU WILL BE ASKED ABOUT YOUR DIET

YOUR EXERCISE PATTERN WILL BE DISCUSSED

RIGHT *Your physician will be able to refer you to a nutritional therapist.*

WHAT TO EXPECT FROM A CONSULTATION

A consultation with a nutritional therapist normally takes up to an hour, during which time he or she takes a full case history. This will include looking at your diet, habits (including how much alcohol you drink or how much you smoke), exercise patterns, emotional and physical history, whether or not you take any medication or drugs, such as the contraceptive pill, as well as any physical symptoms that you may be experiencing.

At the consultation, three basic diagnoses are made by the nutritional therapist: allergy (or intolerance), nutritional deficiencies (usually subclinical), and toxic overload.

Many practitioners suggest a hair, urine, and sweat analysis, muscle testing, and perhaps a questionnaire to pinpoint specific nutritional deficiencies. Further therapy will be based on your physical symptoms. A diet plan will be produced for you, and any supplementation will be prescribed. Exercise and herbal treatment may also be recommended and you may be referred to another complementary or conventional therapist. The number of therapy sessions required depends on how quickly you respond to treatment, how long you have suffered from your symptoms or illness, and how carefully you incorporate the lifestyle and dietary changes suggested.

THE PRACTITIONERS

• Nutritional therapists are complementary medical practitioners who use special diets and a wide variety of nutritional products to enhance or repair specific metabolic functions that may be causing ill-health. They will be trained in biochemistry, physiology, pathology, nutrition, and the principles of naturopathy. A nutritional therapist uses a wide variety of laboratory tests for nutritional deficiencies.

• Dieticians are trained in conventional, state-regulated nutrition, and will have at their disposal treatments and diagnostic techniques available to the conventional medical establishment. Dieticians are not physicians, but they may be trained as nurses.

• Clinical nutritionists are specialist medical physicians who are specifically trained in nutrition (most physicians receive only a little training on nutrition at medical school), and who have studied in a traditional medical establishment. Clinical nutrition is now considered to be a complementary therapy, but many of the practitioners have conventional beliefs.

BELOW *Some nutritional therapists may prescribe herbal remedies as well as nutritional supplements.*

ABOVE *Nutritional therapists work outside the traditional medical establishment.*

ABOVE *Clinical nutritionists are medical physicians with specialized training in nutrition.*

ABOVE *Dieticians are trained in conventional, state-regulated nutrition. They are often nurses.*

Managing Your Treatment

ONCE YOU HAVE DECIDED to take nutritional supplements, or have had them prescribed by a therapist, you need to plan how and when to take them. Some supplements are best taken with food, others on an empty stomach; some once a day, others two or three times. Always follow the advice you are given. You should begin to see results within a few weeks.

Always follow instructions for treatment carefully, as suggested by your nutritional practitioner. Some supplements are best taken on an empty stomach, and others will be completely absorbed by the body only when there is food present. Treatment will always be based on your individual needs, and what works for another person may not be appropriate for you.

Follow the doses prescribed for you by a practitioner, or provided on the back of a supplement carton. While we are encouraged to eat as much healthy food as possible, for its therapeutic benefits and nutrient content, the same does not follow for supplementation. More is not better, and taking extra of any one supplement can seriously upset the balance of the body and result in deficiencies of other nutrients. Where dosages are set at therapeutic levels, for various health or lifestyle conditions, these should not be exceeded, and should only be taken for a short period of time – say two or three weeks – until the condition has either resolved or improved to such an extent that the "picture" has changed, and your requirements will be different.

GRAPEFRUIT IS A GOOD SOURCE OF VITAMIN C AND POTASSIUM

BANANAS ARE HIGH IN POTASSIUM

TOMATOES ARE RICH IN VITAMIN E

APPLES ARE A GOOD SOURCE OF VITAMIN C AND FIBER

LEMONS ARE RICH IN VITAMIN C

CARROTS ARE AN EXCELLENT SOURCE OF BETA-CAROTENE

ABOVE We are encouraged to eat as much fruit and vegetables as possible, but with supplementation, more is not necessarily better.

COMBINE SUPPLEMENTS WITH OTHER THERAPIES?

Vitamins, minerals, and other elements of nutrition are, in essence, simply parts of food, so they are safe to take with other medication and with complementary treatments. (Indeed most good complementary therapies offer advice on nutrition as part of their treatment, since a nutritious diet forms the basis of health on the most fundamental level.) Some therapies, such as herbalism, use herbs and other plant products for nutritional as well as medicinal purposes, and you should tell your practitioner if you are taking supplements, since the action can be duplicated and you may well be taking too much of one thing. It is sensible always to tell your physician or therapist if you are taking supplements and they will advise you if there are likely to be contraindications.

HOW LONG WILL IT TAKE TO WORK?

Marginal deficiencies will often be righted in a short period of time, and you should begin to see effects within a few weeks. Righting deficiency should not take long, and you should not expect to have to take extra supplements, or large doses of any vitamins and minerals, for much longer than several months. However, there are cases where your individual lifestyle, eating habits, body chemistry, and metabolism will increase your needs for nutrients. For example, if you

ABOVE *Boost your vitamin C intake with fresh citrus fruits, particularly if you smoke or are under stress.*

smoke, you will need to take extra vitamin C, and B-complex vitamins, as well as the antioxidants, on a regular basis. If you have a gut absorption problem, you may need to take supplements until the condition is righted.

Some people with chronic health problems may need to take a series of different supplements on an on-going basis.

Generally speaking, however, you should begin to see results within two to three weeks of beginning supplementation. If not, the chances are that it is not doing any good.

Governments around the world have provided guidelines for how much of each vitamin or mineral we need in our diets – R.D.A.s and R.N.I. These are levels of "adequate" intake and do not reflect new thinking on nutrition for optimum health and longevity. In other words, they are not therapeutic levels and they do not take into account the varying needs of the population. People with illnesses, a stressful lifestyle, who are on medication, or eat a highly refined diet, may need much more than the R.D.A. or R.N.I.

BELOW *People who smoke will need to take extra vitamin C, B-complex vitamins, and antioxidants.*

ABOVE *If you have a stressful lifestyle, you may find that you need more vitamin intake than the R.D.A. or R.N.I. recommendation.*

The Listings

VITAMINS ARE COMPOUNDS *needed by the body in small quantities to enable our bodies to grow, develop, and function. They work with enzymes in the body, and other compounds, to help produce energy, build tissues, remove waste, and insure that each system works effectively and efficiently. Minerals are metals and other inorganic compounds that work in much the same way as vitamins, promoting body processes and providing much of the structure for teeth and bones. Minerals are classified in two groups. Proper, or major minerals, are needed in quantities of over 100mg per day, and include calcium, phosphorus, potassium, sodium, chloride, magnesium, and sulfur. Minor minerals, or trace elements, are required by the body in quantities less than 100mg per day, and include chromium, zinc, selenium, silicon, boron, copper, manganese, molybdenum, and vanadium.*

ABOVE *Fresh organic vegetables and fruits contain rich supplies of vitamins and minerals.*

With a few exceptions (such as vitamin D, which can be synthesized by our bodies), the nutrients we need cannot be produced by the body and must be obtained from foods and supplements.

Over the past decades, vitamin and mineral supplementation has been enhanced by a wide variety of other health-giving supplements, many with vitamin-like activities, such as coenzyme Q10, essential fatty acids, amino acids, and herbs. Herbs formed the basis of our first medicines and, in fact, are used today by many pharmaceutical companies as the active ingredient in many prescription and over-the-counter drugs. Herbs are not only nutritious, but they also have a host of therapeutic properties that work to balance and promote health in the body. They are used to help fight infection and disease, and to reduce the damage of free radicals (see pp. 18–19), as well as to improve the action of the various systems of the body, including the immune system, the nervous system and brain, circulatory system, respiratory system, reproductive system, hormones, and the urinary and digestive systems. If you plan to take large doses of vitamins or minerals, consult your physician or nutritionist for advice.

ABOVE *The nutrients that our body needs may be taken in supplement form.*

RIGHT *Medicinal herbs, such as ginkgo biloba, are widely available as supplements.*

How to Use this Section

In the following pages, the most important vitamins and minerals are laid out, with natural sources listed. The symptoms of deficiencies are described, along with the functions of each vitamin or mineral in our bodies. The recommended dosage of each supplement is also given.

Each page gives full details of particular supplements, their properties, and dosages.

As well as vitamins and minerals, this section includes details of naturally occurring beneficial elements.

The Listings are fully illustrated throughout with clear, explanatory color photographs.

Caution boxes warn against any potential harmful effects that may be experienced by particular groups of people.

ABOVE **Throughout the Listings, all nutritional supplements – their sources, properties, functions, and dosages – are fully explained.**

RECOMMENDED INTAKES

In the U. S. a Food and Nutrition Board has been working since 1940 in order to determine vitamin and mineral requirements. The board regularly issues a brochure which lists the Recommended Dietary Allowances (R.D.A.) of vitamins and other nutrients.

R.D.A. figures are estimations; particular requirements will be less or more, depending on individual factors, such as environmental influences, genetics, and presence or absence of disease processes.

In Europe and the U.K., the R.N.I. – Reference Nutrient Intake – is used, which represents the amount of a nutrient that is deemed by the government to be sufficient to meet the needs of almost all healthy people – even those with higher than average requirements. In the U.K., this figure is roughly the same as the old R.D.A. (Recommended Daily Amount), which was formerly the only set of figures used.

The E.A.R., or Estimated Average Requirement, is the amount of a nutrient considered sufficient to meet

the needs of an average, healthy person. The L.R.N.I., or the Lower Reference Nutrient Intake, represents the amount of a nutrient almost certain to be inadequate. For example, the average intake of the trace element selenium in the U.K. falls well below this figure.

S.A.I., or Safe Adequate Intake, is figure given for vitamins and minerals that do not have set R.N.I., R.D.A., or E.A.R. values. It indicates what is considered to be a safe level on a daily basis.

Vitamin A

RETINOL AND BETA-CAROTENE

Retinol is the naturally occurring form of vitamin A, and it is found mainly in animal products. Beta-carotene, also called "plant" vitamin A, is, in fact, a carotenoid, which is converted into vitamin A by our livers. Beta-carotene is found in all brightly colored fruits and vegetables, and is generally believed to be safer than retinol, which is fat-soluble.

RIGHT *Apricots are a good source of beta-carotene and may help boost immunity.*

DATA FILE

U.K. R.N.I. *700mcg (2,300iu)* **U.S. R.D.A.** *1,000mcg (3,300iu)*

Vitamin A is a fat-soluble vitamin, and in its naturally occurring (preformed) form, it is known as retinol. Retinol is found mainly in animal products, and it will be metabolized better by your body if you take it with fat, oil, or protein in the same meal. Vitamin A stores in your body can be depleted by infection, so it is a good idea to boost your intake during colds, flu, and other viral or bacterial conditions.

- Boosts immunity
- Helps to prevent cancer
- Antiaging
- Necessary for healthy eyesight, mucous membranes, synthesis of protein, and tissue development

Deficiency symptoms
Poor vision (night blindness), mouth ulcers, frequent infections, dandruff, and acne.

Good sources
Of retinol: liver, fish-liver oils, cheese, butter.
Of beta-carotene: carrots, apricots, cantaloupe, parsley, spinach, kale, sweet potatoes.

Therapeutic uses
Acne, psoriasis, eyesight problems, cold and flu prevention, gastric ulcers.

SPECIAL NOTES

❖ Retinol in very high doses may cause headaches, some nausea, and liver problems. Pregnant women, or those planning a pregnancy, should not take in excess of 7,500iu per day because it can cause birth defects. They should also avoid eating animal livers.

❖ Beta-carotene, a carotenoid, is converted into vitamin A by the liver, and is known as provitamin A.

❖ Carotenoids are pigments that give plants their color, and beta-carotene in particular is a good antioxidant (*see pp. 18–19*), which may help to slow down the aging process and prevent cancer.

❖ It is a good idea to take vitamins E and C with vitamin A, since polyunsaturated fatty acids work against vitamin A unless there are antioxidants present.

❖ Women on the contraceptive pill require less vitamin A.

❖ The body needs zinc to utilize stored vitamin A.

BELOW *Deficiency symptoms may appear if your vitamin A stores are depleted.*

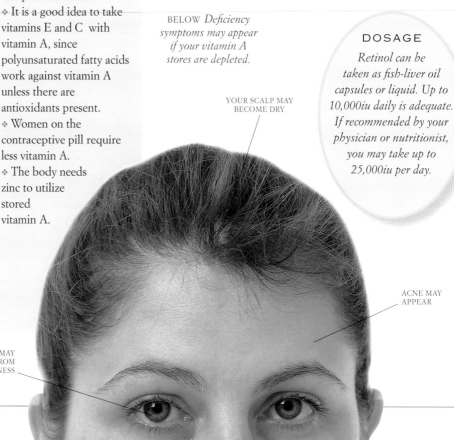

YOUR SCALP MAY BECOME DRY

ACNE MAY APPEAR

THE EYES MAY SUFFER FROM NIGHT BLINDNESS

DOSAGE

Retinol can be taken as fish-liver oil capsules or liquid. Up to 10,000iu daily is adequate. If recommended by your physician or nutritionist, you may take up to 25,000iu per day.

Vitamin B1

THIAMINE

Vitamin B1, or thiamine, is a water-soluble vitamin, which means that it is not stored in the body. A member of the B-complex family, it is necessary for the functioning of the nervous system. Thiamine is easily destroyed by air, water, caffeine, alcohol, estrogen, and food additives, so it is necessary to eat fresh, whole foods in order to get optimum levels of this important vitamin. All of the B-complex vitamins should be taken in combination for best effect.

DOSAGE

Usually 50mg is adequate, although your practitioner may recommend higher doses for therapeutic purposes. The best supplements are those that contain all of the B vitamins.

ABOVE *Vitamin B1 may be destroyed by drinks that contain caffeine, such as coffee.*

BELOW *Insure that you eat plenty of foods rich in thiamine, for example, oatmeal.*

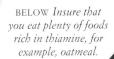

DATA FILE

U.K. R.N.I. *1mg* U.S. R.D.A. *1.5mg*

Like all B-complex vitamins, thiamine is water soluble, which means that the body does not store it. Thiamine is also the least stable of the vitamins, and cooking and processing cause massive losses to occur. Caffeine, alcohol, air, water, estrogen, and sulfur drugs and food additives are antithiamine factors, or "enemies." It is known as the "morale vitamin" because of its effect on mental outlook and the nervous system in general.

- Necessary for the production of energy, and for brain, muscle, heart, and nervous-system function
- Necessary for the conversion of carbohydrates to energy
- Improves mental state
- Promotes growth

Deficiency symptoms
The most common deficiency symptom is beriberi, and long-term deficiency can take a great time to put right, even when the diet is altered to supply adequate amounts.

Good sources
Dried yeast, beans, wholegrains, oatmeal, pork, vegetables, milk, brown rice.

Therapeutic uses
Postoperative pain, treatment of the herpes zoster virus (shingles), epilepsy, trigeminal neuralgia, and sensory neuropathy in diabetics.

SPECIAL NOTES

❖ Vitamin B1 is not toxic in any known quantities and is one of the safest of the vitamins.
❖ Foods that claim to be thiamine-enriched are likely to contain less than normal quantities, since the thiamine lost in processing is usually more than the quantity added.
❖ The B vitamins are synergistic, which means that they work together.

Insure that you take vitamins B1, B2, and B6 in roughly equal quantities.
❖ A folic-acid deficiency, and eating large quantities of raw fish, blackcurrants, and red cabbage, among others, will discourage thiamine metabolism.
❖ Smoking, alcohol, the contraceptive pill, and a diet high in sugar will increase requirements.

Vitamin B2

RIBOFLAVIN

Stress increases our need for riboflavin, vitamin B2, and during periods of emotional or physical pressure, you will need to insure that you increase your intake. Like the other B vitamins, riboflavin is water-soluble and easily antagonized by substances such as caffeine, alcohol, estrogen, and, in this case, zinc.

ABOVE *B2 is necessary for healthy skin, hair, and nails – but too much alcohol and coffee will destroy this vitamin.*

DOSAGE

Usually 50mg is adequate, although your practitioner may recommend higher doses for therapeutic purposes. The best supplements are those that contain all of the B vitamins.

DATA FILE

U.K. R.N.I. *1.3mg* U.S. R.D.A. *1.7mg*

Vitamin B2, riboflavin, is a water-soluble vitamin that is easily absorbed by the body. It is far more stable than thiamine, although it can be destroyed by excess zinc, antibiotics, estrogen, caffeine, and alcohol. Sunlight can also destroy riboflavin, which is why milk cartons are made from opaque materials.

- Aids growth
- Promotes skin, hair, and nail health
- Necessary for metabolism of fats, proteins, and carbohydrates
- Necessary for reproduction
- Activates vitamin B6
- Converts carbohydrates to energy

Deficiency symptoms
Sore mouth, lips, and tongue, insomnia, photosensitivity, bloodshot, gritty eyes, scaly red skin on the sides of the nose. Stress increases your need for riboflavin.

Good sources
Milk, liver, eggs, meat, leafy green vegetables, yeast, fish, wholegrains.

Therapeutic uses
Some anemias, cataracts, poor skin, vision problems (in particular eye fatigue), acne rosacea and other skin problems, carpal tunnel syndrome.

LEFT *Include milk and eggs in your diet to insure that you have an adequate supply of vitamin B2.*

SPECIAL NOTES

❖ Riboflavin is not toxic at any known level. However, some minor symptoms of excessive riboflavin include mild numbness and itching and burning sensations.

❖ Your needs will increase if you are pregnant, on the contraceptive pill, breast-feeding, or if you have a diet that is low in meat and dairy produce.

❖ Like thiamine, riboflavin requires other B vitamins to work most effectively.

Vitamin B3

NIACIN

The third member of the B-complex family of vitamins is niacin, vitamin B3. Niacin is vital for normal brain function, and deficiency has been linked to schizophrenia and depression. Smaller deficiencies of this vitamin may be responsible for insomnia, fatigue, and mouth ulcers, for example. Vitamin B3 also improves the health of the skin, the circulation, and the digestive system. Do not supplement vitamin B3 above daily doses of 100mg, unless supervised by a registered practitioner.

SPECIAL NOTES

❖ Alcohol inhibits the metabolism of niacin, and sleeping pills, estrogen, and food processing will destroy the vitamin.

❖ Niacin is essentially nontoxic, although doses above 100mg can cause side effects including the "niacin flush," characterized by burning, itching skin. Some studies indicate that doses higher than 500mg can cause some liver damage.

❖ The niacin flush may be exacerbated by taking antibiotics.

❖ Niacin is available in two forms – niacin, or nicotinic acid, and niacinamide, or nictinamide.

BELOW *Avocados are an excellent source of vitamin B3 and will guard against any possible deficiency.*

DOSAGE

Take as part of a good B-complex supplement, and increase your intake if you are pregnant, breast-feeding, on the contraceptive pill, or in your childbearing years. 100mg is usually adequate, although higher doses may be recommended therapeutically.

DATA FILE

U.K. R.N.I. *18mg* U.S. R.D.A. *19mg*

Niacin is a water-soluble vitamin, and it is essential for normal brain function. Many cases of schizophrenia and depression have been linked to a niacin deficiency. Women of childbearing age are likely to require more niacin, since estrogens inhibit the conversion of tryptophan to vitamin B3. If you suffer from B-vitamin deficiencies you cannot produce niacin from tryptophan.

- Necessary for synthesis of sex hormones, and cortisone, thyroxin, and insulin
- Improves circulation
- Health of skin, nerves, brain, and digestive system
- Required for the synthesis of D.N.A.
- Converts carbohydrates to energy

Deficiency symptoms
Insomnia, T.A.T. (Tired All the Time syndrome), poor appetite, digestive problems, muscle weakness, irritability, skin problems, mouth sores, and psychiatric disturbances.

Good sources
Liver, lean meats, wholegrains, peanuts, fish, eggs, avocados, sunflower seeds, prunes.

Therapeutic uses
Menstrual pain and irregularity, skin problems, migraine headaches, circulatory problems, high blood pressure, vertigo in Ménière's syndrome, mouth ulcers, high cholesterol, tinnitus, some types of diabetes, and wheezing in asthmatics.

BELOW *Eating sunflower seeds and prunes will boost your levels of vitamin B3.*

Vitamin B5

PANTOTHENIC ACID

Pantothenic acid, or vitamin B5, is also a member of the B-complex family of vitamins. It is one of the safest of all vitamins and, like riboflavin, is helpful in times of stress. Because it is essential for the conversion of carbohydrates in our diet to energy, even a slight deficiency can lead to fatigue.

B5 IS GOOD FOR DEPRESSION

TIREDNESS IS A SIGN OF B5 DEFICIENCY

BELOW *Vitamin B5 can help prevent stress-related illnesses by producing antistress hormones.*

SKIN DISORDERS MAY RESPOND TO B5 SUPPLEMENTS

DOSAGE

Up to 500mg daily can be used for immune problems and arthritis (taken with an equal amount of vitamin C). Pantothenic acid is normally found in vitamin B-complex formulas, in amounts of between 10mg and 100mg. It is recommended that you get up to 300mg daily, in food or supplementally.

BELOW *Food processing destroys vitamin B5, so avoid canned food if you require this vitamin.*

SPECIAL NOTES

❖ Vitamin B5 is one of the safest of the vitamins, with no known side effects or toxic levels.

❖ Extra pantothenic acid can help to prevent stress-related illnesses.

Vitamin B6

PYRIDOXINE

Deficiency of pyridoxine, or vitamin B6, is most common in those of us who eat diets centered around "junk" or "convenience" foods. Food processing destroys up to 90 percent of vitamin B6 content of any food, which means that whole, fresh foods are the key natural source. Many menstrual problems, including P.M.S., are also linked to small deficiencies of this vitamin.

DOSAGE

Take as part of a good B-complex supplement, with equal amounts of vitamin B1 and B2. Doses up to 100 to 200mg per day are safe; it is not recommended that you take in excess of 500mg daily.

ABOVE *Supplement your intake of B6 by eating bananas.*

SPECIAL NOTES

❖ In the U.K. it is planned to limit quantities of B6 sold separately and in multivitamin form to 10mg per tablet, over and above which a prescription would be required. This action is being fiercely debated at the time of going to press.

❖ Arthritis sufferers taking penicillamine will require B6 supplements.

❖ Canning, roasting, heat processing, water, alcohol, and estrogen all destroy vitamin B6.

❖ B6 should not be taken by anyone undergoing levodopa treatment for Parkinson's disease.

❖ Taking doses of over 2 to 10g can cause neurological disorders.

DATA FILE

U.K. R.N.I. *1.5mg* U.S. R.D.A. *2.2mg*

Vitamin B6 is another of the water-soluble vitamins, and any excess is normally excreted from the body about eight hours after ingestion. Because of this, and because up to 90 percent of the vitamin is destroyed through food processing, deficiency is quite common. Vitamin B6 is also known as pyridoxine, pyridoxinal, and pyridoxamine, all of which are related substances. Pyridoxine is the most commonly used form of vitamin B6. Women taking Hormone Replacement Therapy (H.R.T.) or the contraceptive pill will have increased requirements. So too will people with diets high in protein or with an excessive alcohol consumption.

- Necessary for the production of hydrochloric acid and magnesium
- Necessary for absorption of vitamin B12
- Necessary for the production of antibodies and red blood cells
- Metabolizes protein, carbohydrates, and fats
- Helps metabolize and transport selenium
- Natural diuretic
- Helps the body to absorb zinc
- Alleviates nausea
- Promotes synthesis of nucleic acids

Deficiency symptoms
Anemia, insomnia, kidney stones, morning sickness, premenstrual syndrome (P.M.S.), skin rashes and dry skin, nervousness, and infant convulsions.

Good sources
Avocados, bananas, fish, wheat bran, liver, cantaloupe, cabbage, milk, eggs, seeds.

Therapeutic uses
Night muscle spasms, leg cramps, hand numbness, morning sickness, skin and nervous disorders, insulin resistance, P.M.S., carpal tunnel syndrome, asthma, kidney stones, anemia, fluid retention, childhood autism, heart disease.

RIGHT *Alcohol destroys vitamin B6; insure that you do not drink excessively.*

Folic Acid

VITAMIN BC

Folic acid, a member of the B-complex family of vitamins, is sometimes known as vitamin Bc. We know now that folic acid is crucial to the development of the fetus, and experts advise that this vitamin be taken preconceptually and during pregnancy to reduce the risk of birth defects. Folic acid is easily destroyed by cooking, processing, and exposure to light and air. If you are a heavy drinker, you may need to increase your intake.

LEFT *If you suffer from nervous disorders, be sure to include foods rich in folic acid in your diet, including melons.*

SPECIAL NOTES

❖ Pregnant women are recommended to take 400mcg per day; doses above that are not recommended unless under the supervision of a registered practitioner. It may cause problems with zinc absorption.

❖ Increase your intake if you are a heavy drinker.

❖ Take extra folic acid when you are fighting an illness, or if you have an immune condition.

❖ Increase folic acid intake if you take more than 2g of vitamin C daily.

❖ Folic acid is not toxic, although in very high doses (more than about 2,000mcg) some people experience skin rashes.

DOSAGE

400mcg to 800mcg is usually adequate for most people's needs, although up to 5mg is considered to be safe when recommended by a registered practitioner. B-complex tablets do not usually contain an adequate amount, and if your diet does not have plenty of folic acid, you may need to supplement.

DATA FILE

U.K. R.N.I. *200mcg* U.S. R.D.A. *200mcg*

Folic acid is a water-soluble vitamin, generally considered to be one of the B-complex family. Recently, folic acid has been identified as being crucial to the development of the fetus, and helps to prevent spina bifida when taken preconceptually and prenatally. Folic acid is easily destroyed by cooking and by food processing, and it is sensitive to light. If you take the contraceptive pill, antiepileptic drugs, antacids, excess alcohol, or aspirin, or if you have a zinc or vitamin B12 deficiency, you will most probably need to increase your intake of folic acid.

- Essential for division of body cells
- Required for utilization of sugar and amino acids, particularly glycine and methionine
- Folic acid is necessary for the production of nucleic acids
- Necessary for red-blood-cell formation

Deficiency symptoms
Nervous problems, impaired memory, difficulty lactating while breast-feeding, insomnia, confusion, reduced immunity, recurrent miscarriage, breathlessness, anorexia, fatigue, digestive problems, increased risk of cancer and heart disease, and birth defects, particularly spina bifida.

Good sources
Leafy green vegetables, carrots, liver, egg yolk, apricots, avocados, beans, whole wheat, melons, fresh oranges.

Therapeutic uses
Some anemias, cervical dysplasia, immune problems, food poisoning and intestinal parasites (which it protects against), depression, skin problems, convalescence, mouth ulcers, pain (it acts as an analgesic).

RIGHT *Insure that you take folic acid leading up to conception and during pregnancy to help prevent spina bifida from developing in your unborn baby.*

Vitamin B12

COBALAMIN

Vitamin B12, or cobalamin, is a member of the B-complex family, occurring naturally in animal products, including milk and cheese. B12 needs calcium for proper assimilation, and deficiency may give rise to anemia, among other things. Although we need very little vitamin B12, our absorption is often inadequate, and vegans, in particular, may need to take supplements. Like vitamin B1, B12 is known as a "feel-good" vitamin, as it helps insure the healthy functioning of the nervous system.

SPECIAL NOTES

❖ Sunlight, water, alcohol, estrogen, and sleeping pills all act as "enemies" toward vitamin B12.

❖ A time-release tablet is often recommended since B12 is not well absorbed through the stomach, and this offers the opportunity for it to be absorbed in the small intestine.

❖ Symptoms of B12 deficiency may take more than five years to show up.

❖ Chronic diarrhea, intestinal parasites, and other digestive disorders can inhibit the absorption of B12, and deficiency is particularly common in the elderly.

❖ There are no reported cases of toxicity, and B12 appears to be safe at any dosage level.

❖ Many women find B12 useful for the symptoms of P.M.S., and for menstrual problems in general.

❖ Paradoxically, diets rich in protein may require extra B12 – the more B12 ingested, the lower the percentage of absorption.

DATA FILE

U.K. R.N.I. *1.5mcg* U.S. R.D.A. *3mcg*

Vitamin B12, also called cobalamin and cyanocobalamin, is known as the "red vitamin." It is water soluble and found only in animal foods, although some vegetarian foods are now fortified with additional B12. Vitamin B12 is the only vitamin that contains essential minerals, and our needs are fairly small. However, it is not easily assimilated when taken orally, and it needs to be combined with calcium to be properly absorbed. In many cases, an injection is the best form in which to take supplemental vitamin B12, particularly where there are absorption problems.

- Forms and regenerates red blood cells
- Essential for a healthy nervous system
- Essential for growth and development
  - Vitamin B12 is necessary to utilize fats, proteins, and carbohydrates
- Improves concentration, memory, and balance
- Detoxifies cyanide from foods and tobacco smoke

Deficiency symptoms
Anemia, fatigue, heart disease, brain damage, nerve damage, a sore tongue, and hallucination.

Good sources
Liver, beef, cheese, milk, kidneys, yogurt, eggs.

Therapeutic uses
Appetite problems, convalescence, chronic fatigue, confusion and dementia, tinnitus, multiple sclerosis, chronic pain, irritability.

BELOW *B12 occurs naturally only in animal products, such as liver.*

DOSAGE

Supplements of between 50 and 2,000mcg have been reported safe, and injections are routinely offered by physicians. Daily doses are usually between 10 and 100mcg, and should be taken with vitamins C, E, and A, and the other members of the B-complex family.

Vitamin C

ASCORBIC ACID

Vitamin C is one of the most important vitamins for the immune system, and for the health of every tissue in the body. Because vitamin C is water-soluble, our bodies are unable to store it, and we must insure that we get adequate quantities in our diets on a regular basis. The best forms of this vitamin are fruits and vegetables, which should be eaten fresh, or raw, whenever possible.

DATA FILE

U.K. R.N.I. *40mg*   U.S. R.D.A. *60mg*

Vitamin C is a water-soluble vitamin, and one of the most important vitamins for the immune system. Humans, apes, and guinea pigs are the only mammals that do not synthesize vitamin C, and we rely on our diets to get all we need. Excess vitamin C is, however, rapidly excreted from the body, and easily lost from foods, particularly when they are boiled, stored for long periods, and exposed to air (for example after cutting). In order to get adequate amounts, we must eat at least four to five servings of fresh, lightly steamed, or raw fruits and vegetables daily.

Alcohol, aspirin, tobacco, stress, infections, and the contraceptive pill all lead to an increased need for vitamin C, and it is recommended that anyone who smokes or drinks heavily should have up to 400mg per day above normal requirements.

- Necessary for the absorption of iron
- Antioxidant
- Stimulates activity of the immune system
- Encourages production of stress hormones
- Helps wounds to heal
- Necessary for healthy bones and tissue
- Necessary for the growth and repair of blood vessels, cells, gums, bones, and teeth

Deficiency symptoms
Bleeding, sore gums and loose teeth, fatigue, lowered immune activity, bruising, hypoglycemia, and blood and skin problems.

Good sources
Citrus fruits, broccoli, tomatoes, cauliflower, potatoes, leafy green vegetables, green bell peppers, Brussels sprouts, cabbage.

Therapeutic uses
Healing wounds and burns, decreasing blood cholesterol levels, treating asthma, preventing and curing colds and other infectious illnesses, preventing, treating, and sometimes curing some forms of cancer, encouraging immune activity, lowering incidence of blood clots in the veins, reducing effects of many allergens, for manic depression, blood-sugar problems, toxic conditions, aging, degenerative disease.

VITAMIN C ENCOURAGES IMMUNE ACTIVITY

VITAMIN C DECREASES THE INTENSITY AND DURATION OF A COLD OR FLU

LEFT *Vitamin C boosts the immune system and may help to prevent colds and other infectious illnesses.*

CABBAGE

RED BELL PEPPER

GREEN BELL PEPPER

BRUSSELS SPROUTS

CAULIFLOWER

BROCCOLI

RIGHT *Broccoli, leafy green vegetables, green bell peppers, and Brussels sprouts are all good sources of vitamin C.*

SPECIAL NOTES

❖ Vitamin C is not toxic, although excessive intake may cause diarrhea and some skin rashes.

❖ Vitamin C can alter the results of blood and urine tests, including those for diabetes. Let your physician know if you are taking supplemental vitamin C.

❖ Vitamin C works best with bioflavonoids *(see p. 85)*, calcium, and magnesium.

❖ Carbon monoxide destroys vitamin C, so anyone living in polluted areas will have increased requirements.

❖ Insure that you do not supplement more than 1g daily if you take the contraceptive pill, since estrogen and vitamin C require the same excretive mechanisms in the body.

❖ Excessive intake can interfere with the absorption of other vitamins and minerals, so if you are taking high doses, insure that you do so between meals.

❖ If you regularly take high doses and intend to cut down, do so gradually to insure that deficiency symptoms do not appear.

❖ Vitamin C can be taken in a number of forms such as powder or granules, tablets, and capsules.

❖ Vitamin C powders are less irritating to the digestive system, and will help to prevent diarrhea, which can be associated with excess amounts.

❖ Time-release tablets are the most effective, since the body so rapidly excretes any excess.

❖ Research shows that dosages of 1,000mg to 3,000mg can be safely maintained, and it is useful to sustain high levels of vitamin C in the tissues on an on-going basis.

ABOVE *Vitamin C is destroyed by carbon monoxide so people living in polluted areas should increase their intake.*

DOSAGE

Many experts suggest that you take 1g daily as a preventive measure, particularly since so much of our food is low in vitamin C because of storage, processing, and farming methods. Daily doses are usually from 500mg to 4g.

LEFT *Boost your daily intake of vitamin C with tasty and nutritious fresh citrus fruits and juices.*

Vitamin E

ALPHA TOCOPHEROL

Vitamin E is an antioxidant vitamin, with a wide range of therapeutic uses. Although this vitamin is fat-soluble, it is stored less efficiently by the body than most, and very vulnerable to processing: 90 percent is, for example, lost when wheat is refined into white flour. Smokers and women who take the contraceptive pill have additional vitamin E requirements.

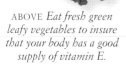

ABOVE *Eat fresh green leafy vegetables to insure that your body has a good supply of vitamin E.*

DOSAGE

Dosages of between 200 and 300iu per day are usually considered to be adequate, although smokers, pregnant and breast-feeding women, and women of menopause age will require more. Used therapeutically, vitamin E can be safely taken in doses up to 1,000 to 2,000iu daily, although most practitioners don't recommend taking more than 1,000iu daily.

LEFT *Regular use of vitamin E skin cream helps to slow down the degenerative aging process.*

DATA FILE

U.K. R.N.I. *none* **U.S. R.D.A.** *15iu*

Vitamin E is a fat-soluble vitamin, but unlike other fat-soluble vitamins, up to 70 percent of intake is excreted in the feces each day. It is stored in the liver, fatty tissues, heart, testes, uterus, muscles, blood, and the adrenal and pituitary glands. Vitamin E is chemically known as alpha tocopherol, the most active of a group of eight tocopherols. It has a huge number of therapeutic properties and is used in the treatment of many health disorders, including coronary artery disease, muscular dystrophy, habitual spontaneous abortion, and schizophrenia. It has also been used successfully in the treatment and prevention of some cancers.

Smokers and women taking the contraceptive pill will need extra vitamin E, since both are reported to lead to deficiency. Vitamin E is easily destroyed by heat, oxygen, freezing, food processing, and chlorine (found in some drinking water). Frozen foods, particularly those that have been frozen for longer than two months, are likely to have negligible vitamin E content.

- Slows the aging process
- Provides the body with oxygen
- Antioxidant
- Protects lungs against pollution
- Helps the development and maintenance of nerves and muscles
- Helps to prevent miscarriages
- Improves immune activity in the body
- Works as a natural diuretic
- Heals the skin, and helps to prevent scarring
- Improves fertility
- Reduces oxygen requirements of muscles

Deficiency symptoms
Muscle degeneration, reproductive problems, some anemias, age spots, cataracts, infertility, fragile red blood cells, and some neuromuscular damage.

Good sources
Wheatgerm, soybeans, vegetable oils, broccoli, leafy green vegetables, whole wheat, eggs, oats, almonds, butter, peanuts, sunflower oil, seeds.

Therapeutic uses
Burns, delays progress of Parkinson's disease, reduces risk of heart attack in people who have heart disease, reduces effects of pollution, encourages insulin action in diabetics, P.M.S., osteoarthritis, helps control epileptic seizures, for gangrene, immune-system problems including autoimmune disorders, cystic breast disease, fertility problems, pain of shingles and other neuralgias, some cancers, menstrual problems, and, with selenium, muscular dystrophy.

LEFT *Vitamin E supplements are used to reduce the harmful effects of pollution.*

FERTILITY PROBLEMS MAY BE SOLVED WITH VITAMIN E SUPPLEMENTS

INCREASE YOUR INTAKE OF VITAMIN E IF YOU ARE PREGNANT

RIGHT *Pregnant women are advised to increase their intake of vitamin E to help prevent miscarriage.*

SPECIAL NOTES

❖ Vitamin E is essentially nontoxic, and there are no known toxic reactions.

❖ Do not take supplements if you are taking anticoagulants, since vitamin E acts as a natural anticoagulant.

❖ You may experience a temporary rise in blood pressure when supplementing vitamin E, so you should discuss supplementation with your physician if you suffer from high blood pressure.

❖ Inorganic iron, known as ferrous sulfate, destroys vitamin E, and should not be taken within eight hours of taking vitamin E.

❖ Chlorinated drinking water increases vitamin E requirements.

❖ Women of menopause age will require increased vitamin E, as will pregnant or breast-feeding mothers, and women taking the contraceptive pill.

❖ Products with 25mcg of selenium for each 200iu of vitamin E will encourage the efficiency of the vitamin.

❖ Vitamin E can be taken in capsules (as an oil) or in dried form. The dried form is preferred by people who are sensitive or intolerant to oil.

Vitamin D

CALCIFEROL AND ERGOCALCIFEROL

Vitamin D is produced by the body in the presence of sunlight. Because it is fat-soluble, it is stored in the body and deficiency is uncommon. Vitamin D is required for the absorption and metabolism of many minerals, and, in particular, vitamin A. It is also essential for the growth of bones and teeth, and kidney function. Vitamin D can be toxic if it is taken in large quantities.

LEFT *Include oily fish, such as sardines, in your diet if you are concerned about vitamin D deficiency.*

SPECIAL NOTES

❖ Anyone who works at night, or whose clothing (for example in some religions) prevents exposure to the sun, will require extra vitamin D in the diet.

❖ Anyone who lives in highly polluted areas will need to increase their vitamin D intake.

❖ Elderly people are less efficient at synthesizing vitamin D and are likely to need supplementation.

❖ The absorption of supplemental vitamin D is encouraged by eating fats or oils in the same meal.

❖ Vegans, especially those who live in cold climates, are advised to take supplemental vitamin D during the winter months.

❖ Because vitamin D is fat-soluble, large or repeated doses can build up to toxic levels in the body; symptoms may include nausea and vomiting, calcium deposits, unusual thirst, sore eyes, itching skin, kidney damage, damage to the arteries, irregular heartbeat, and high blood pressure.

❖ The most common form of supplementation is natural cod-liver oil, which can be taken in capsule or as an oil.

DATA FILE

U.K. R.N.I. *none*   U.S. R.D.A. *5mcg(200iu)*

Vitamin D is a fat-soluble vitamin, and it can be stored in the body. Vitamin D can also be synthesized (produced) by the body, through sunlight, which acts upon the oils of the skin to produce the vitamin, which is then absorbed into the body. Pollution can inhibit the action of the sunlight on the body, and people who live in areas with high air pollution may not produce adequate amounts. Tanning also makes production of vitamin D less efficient.

Vitamin D produced in the body, or ingested as natural foods, is known as calciferol. Synthetic vitamin D, which is often used in supplements, is known as ergocalciferol. Taken orally, vitamin D is absorbed with fats, through the intestines.

- Necessary for the absorption of magnesium, calcium, zinc, iron, phosphorus, and other minerals
- Helps the body to assimilate vitamin A
- Necessary for the health of the bones and teeth
- Necessary for the metabolism of calcium and phosphorus
- Required for kidney function

Deficiency symptoms
Rickets in children, tooth decay, osteoporosis, and osteomalacia.

Good sources
Milk and dairy products (particularly butter), oily fish, fish-liver oils.

Therapeutic uses
Tooth and bone diseases, prevention of colds, some forms of psoriasis, calcium absorption problems, conjunctivitis, migraine.

DOSAGE

Most capsules contain approximately 400iu (in the form of natural fish-liver oils), and doses of between 400 and 1,000iu can be taken daily. Dosages above 1,000iu daily are not recommended unless under the supervision of a registered practitioner.

BELOW *The human body can produce vitamin D itself if exposed to a sufficient amount of sunlight.*

Vitamin K

PHYLLOQUINONE OR MENAQUINONE, MENADIONE

Vitamin K is an important fat-soluble vitamin, though rarely deficient. Little is stored by the body, but healthy gut bacteria insure adequate amounts of vitamin K. Yogurt, which encourages "healthy" bacterial growth in the intestines, is a good natural source of vitamin K, and can help to prevent deficiency. The main job of vitamin K is to aid blood clotting, and chronic nosebleeds may respond to the therapeutic use of this vitamin.

RIGHT *Supplementation of vitamin K is rarely advised but it is found naturally in foods such as tomatoes.*

DATA FILE

U.K. R.N.I. *none* U.S. R.D.A. *80mcg*

Vitamin K is essential for the liver to synthesize several proteins necessary for the clotting of blood. Chemically, phylloquinone is the natural plant source of vitamin K, and a synthetic derivative, menadione, is used therapeutically. Intestinal bacteria synthesize a family of compounds with vitamin K activity, which are known as menaquinones.

Vitamin K is fat soluble and is stored in the bones and in the liver, but very little is actually laid down. Deficiency of vitamin K rarely occurs. It is used medically in treating specific deficiencies that occur during anticoagulant therapy, and in hemorrhagic disease of the newborn (who have very low vitamin K because they do not have any bacterial activity in the gut).

- Essential for the formation of prothrombin, a blood-clotting chemical
- Required for bone calcification and mineralization

Good sources
Yogurt (live), alfalfa, egg yolks, broccoli, Brussels sprouts, leafy green vegetables, green tea, kelp, wholegrains, liver, tomatoes, fish-liver oils.

Deficiency symptoms
Colon disease, osteoporosis, and bleeding and hemorrhaging.

Therapeutic uses
Excessive menstrual flow, to prevent internal bleeding and blood clotting, to prevent hemorrhagic disease of the newborn.

SPECIAL NOTES

❖ Chronic diarrhea is both a symptom of deficiency and a cause of deficiency, since the vitamin is fat soluble and any problems with fat digestion will discourage its absorption. Anything else that affects the activity of the bowels, including long courses of antibiotics, will also prevent bacterial synthesis.

❖ About 70 percent of dietary vitamin K is excreted daily, so include plenty of vitamin-K-rich foods in your diet.

❖ Yogurt, which encourages the growth of natural bacteria and is a source of vitamin K, is advised for people suffering from deficiency.

❖ Increases the vitamin K content of your diet if you suffer from nosebleeds.

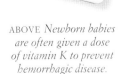

ABOVE *Newborn babies are often given a dose of vitamin K to prevent hemorrhagic disease.*

DOSAGE

Vitamin K is not often supplemented, except in the case of newborn babies. Adequate amounts can be obtained from food. More than 500mcg of synthetic vitamin K (menadione) is not recommended.

Biotin

COENZYME R OR VITAMIN H

Biotin, choline, and inositol are vitamins, or vitamin-like substances, and considered to be part of the B-complex family. Deficiency of any of these vitamins is, however, rare, though they can be used therapeutically. For example, biotin is often used in the treatment of hair loss and premature graying; choline may help to prevent Alzheimer's disease and inositol has been used in the treatment of eczema and a variety of other skin problems.

RIGHT *Biotin supplements may prevent hair from premature graying.*

DATA FILE

U.K. S.A.I. *10–200mcg* **U.S. S.A.I.** *100–200mcg*

Biotin, a complex organic acid containing sulfur, is synthesized by intestinal bacteria and is widespread in food products. It is a water-soluble vitamin, and often considered to be a member of the B-complex family. Biotin is essential for fats and proteins to be metabolized by the body.

- Necessary for the metabolism of proteins, carbohydrates, and fats.
- Necessary for growth, and health of skin, hair, nerves, sex glands, and bone marrow
- Necessary for the metabolism of energy

Deficiency symptoms
A natural deficiency in humans is unusual, but symptoms of deficiency include depression, severe eczema and dermatitis, exhaustion, impairment of fat metabolism, hair loss, premature graying, and anorexia.

Good sources
Meats, dairy produce, wholegrains, liver, egg yolk, nuts, fruits, unpolished rice.

Therapeutic uses
Helps prevent some hair loss and hair from turning prematurely gray, used for muscle pains, eczema, dermatitis, skin problems, some diabetes.

SPECIAL NOTES

❖ There are no known toxic effects of biotin.
❖ Raw egg whites prevent the absorption of biotin.
❖ Long-term use of antibiotics will increase the requirements for biotin, since the body's natural bacteria, necessary for the synthesis of biotin, is destroyed by antibiotics.

❖ Alcohol, food-processing, sulfur drugs, and estrogen all work to destroy biotin.
❖ Biotin works with vitamins B2, B3, B6, and A to maintain healthy skin, and they should be taken together for best effect.

DOSAGE

Biotin is found in most B-complex supplements, and multivitamins and should be taken in doses of between 25 and 300mcg per day. Supplements of up to 1,000mcg may be used therapeutically, under the supervision of a registered practitioner.

RIGHT *Meat, including lamb, will provide an adequate supply of biotin in your diet.*

Choline

$C_5H_{15}NO_2$

Inositol

$C_6H_{12}O_6 2H_2O$

DATA FILE

U.K. R.N.I. *none* U.S. R.D.A. *none*

- Can be synthesized by the body provided that intake of the amino acid methionine is sufficient.
- Helps to remove fat from the liver
- Works to enhance memory
- Helps the nerve impulses to pass, particularly those in the brain used in memory
- Necessary to produce and maintain the structure of cells
- Works with inositol to metabolize fats and cholesterol

Deficiency symptoms
Liver problems, retarded growth, hardening of the arteries, memory problems, and possibly Alzheimer's disease.

Good sources
Egg yolk, brain, heart, nuts, leafy green vegetables, liver, pulses, yeast, lecithin.

Therapeutic uses
High cholesterol, liver problems, depression and anxiety, memory problems (particularly in the elderly), Alzheimer's disease, cirrhosis.

RIGHT *Nuts are a delicious natural source of choline.*

SPECIAL NOTES

❖ Choline should always be taken with other B-vitamins. The best form is phosphatidyl choline, or lecithin.

❖ Always take calcium with choline; it will be required to balance phosphorus and calcium in the body, since choline increases the phosphorus in the body.

DATA FILE

U.K. R.N.I. *None* U.S. R.D.A. *None*

- Necessary for the metabolism of fat and cholesterol
- Necessary for normal brain cell function (and neurotransmitters)
- Helps to remove fat from the liver

Deficiency symptoms
There are no known symptoms of deficiency, although it is believed that eczema may be caused by even mild deficiency.

Good sources
Liver, brewer's yeast, beans, citrus fruit, brains and heart, cantaloupe melon, grapefruit, raisins, wheatgerm, peanuts, cabbage, wholegrains.

Therapeutic uses
High cholesterol levels, hair problems, eczema, depression and anxiety, diabetic neuropathy.

SPECIAL NOTES

❖ There are no known toxic effects of inositol.
❖ Always take calcium with inositol; it will be required to balance phosphorus and calcium in the body, since inositol (and choline) increase the phosphorus in the body.
❖ Inositol should be taken with choline, and other B-vitamins for best effect.

DOSAGES

Most B-complex supplements contain choline and inositol, which are often taken in doses that range between 50 and 1,000mg. Or, take 1–2 tbsp of lecithin daily.

Calcium

CA

Calcium is an essential mineral – it makes up bones and teeth and is also crucial for the transmission of information along the nerves – yet few of us get as much as we need. Women are more often calcium deficient than men, and the elderly, especially elderly women, are particularly vulnerable to lack of calcium. Calcium deficiency can lead to brittle bones, gum disease, and muscle cramps.

ABOVE *The elderly are particularly prone to calcium deficiency.*

DATA FILE

U.K. R.N.I. *700mg* **U.S. R.D.A.** *800mg*

Calcium is an important mineral, and recent research shows that we get only about one-third of what we need for good health. Calcium is essential for human life – it makes up bones and teeth, and is crucial for messages to be conducted along nerves. Almost all of the body's calcium is found in the bones and in the teeth. It insures that our muscles contract, and that our hearts beat, and it is extremely important in the maintenance of the immune system, among other things.

- Necessary for the action of a number of hormones
- Necessary for muscle action
- Required for release of neurotransmitters in the brain, and aids nervous system
- Necessary for blood clotting and blood-pressure regulation
- Maintains strong bones and teeth
- Helps to metabolize iron
- Necessary to keep the heart beating
- Necessary for cell structure
- Helps the body to absorb vitamin B12

Deficiency symptoms
There are many groups at risk of calcium deficiency, particularly the elderly. Because it so important to body processes, our bodies take what they need from our bones, which causes them to become thin and brittle. Parathyroid and thyroid hormones help to maintain proper calcium balance in tissues. A lack of calcium can impair growth and lead to such conditions as rickets and tetany. Other symptoms of deficiency include gum disease, muscles cramping, loss of muscle tone, and convulsions.

Good sources
Milk, cheese, and dairy produce, tofu, leafy green vegetables, salmon, nuts, root vegetables, broccoli.

Therapeutic uses
Growing pains, menstrual cramps, hypoglycemia, muscle cramps, osteoporosis, allergies, high blood pressure, migraine, heart problems, and insomnia.

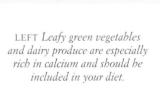
LEFT *Leafy green vegetables and dairy produce are especially rich in calcium and should be included in your diet.*

IF OUR INTAKE IS LOW, CALCIUM NEEDED FOR BODY PROCESSES IS TAKEN FROM OUR BONES

NEEDED FOR HEALTHY TEETH

FRACTURES MAY OCCUR IF THERE IS CALCIUM DEFICIENCY

BONES WILL BECOME THIN AND BRITTLE IF CALCIUM IS DEFICIENT

CALCIUM DEFICIENCY MAY CAUSE RICKETS

SPECIAL NOTES

❖ Doses over 2,000mg per day may cause hypercalcemia, but excess calcium is excreted so that toxic dosage is unlikely.

❖ Calcium and magnesium work together for the health of the heart and circulation. If there is a magnesium deficiency, calcium deficiencies may not respond to supplementation. Take double the amount of calcium as you do magnesium for best effect.

❖ Calcium and phosphorus work together to encourage health of bones and teeth, and should be taken in a two to one ratio (calcium to phosphorus).

❖ Vitamin D is required for calcium absorption.

❖ People on very low-fat diets may have an impaired ability to absorb calcium.

❖ People under stress will have increased requirements, because stress causes calcium to be excreted in the urine at a higher rate.

❖ Women are more vulnerable to calcium deficiency than men.

❖ The best supplemental form of calcium is calcium citrate, which is easily absorbed by the body. Dolomite is less easily absorbed, particularly by people with reduced stomach-acid activity.

DOSAGE

Experts recommend that calcium be taken in a good multivitamin and mineral supplement, although extra doses may be given up to 1,000mg a day.

BELOW *Calcium is needed to promote a healthy nervous system.*

LEFT *Calcium is one of the most important minerals and works within our bodies to create healthy bones and teeth. Deficiency may cause our bones to become thin and brittle.*

Iron

FE

Anemia, the condition often associated with iron deficiency, was first recorded 3,500 years ago. Iron is a component of the red blood cells and the muscles, assisting in the transportation of oxygen throughout the body. Women lose twice as much iron as men, and are more likely to be deficient, particularly during child-bearing years. Drinking coffee within an hour of a meal can reduce iron absorption by up to 80 percent.

LEFT *If you feel that you are lacking in iron, try adding more shellfish, liver, or red meat to your diet.*

BELOW *The physicists of Ancient Egypt recognized iron-deficiency anemia more than 3,500 years ago.*

DATA FILE

U.K. R.N.I. *14.8mg (women); 8.7mg (men)*
U.S. R.D.A. *15mg (women); 10mg (men)*

Iron is an essential mineral nutrient. It is a component of hemoglobin and myoglobin molecules – the hemoglobin in red blood cells transports oxygen from the lungs to body cells and returns waste carbon dioxide from the cells to the lungs. The myoglobin in red muscle tissues transports oxygen into the tissues for energy storage. Iron is also a component of certain metabolic enzymes. Iron in the body that is not in use is stored in the spleen, bone marrow, and liver. Iron-deficiency anemia, which is the condition most commonly associated with deficiency, was described by Egyptian physicists as long ago as 1500 B.C.E. Today, more than 500 million people around the world suffer from this condition. On the average, women lose about twice as much iron as men, and therefore women are most often iron deficient.

- Necessary for production of hemoglobin and certain enzymes
- Necessary for immune activity
- Required to supply oxygen to the cells
- Required by the liver
- Protects against some free radicals *(see pp. 18–19)*

Deficiency symptoms
Anemia, growth problems, some forms of deafness, pallor, breathlessness, tiredness, and reduced bone density.

Good sources
Liver, kidney, raw clams, cocoa powder, beans, dark chocolate, shellfish, nuts, pulses, broccoli, red meat, egg yolks, molasses.

Therapeutic uses
Anemia, hearing loss, menstrual pain, restless leg syndrome, growth problems, poor resistance to infection, fatigue.

DOSAGE

Increased levels of iron may be required by infants, children, athletes, or vegetarians; also women who are pregnant, breast-feeding, or menstruating. Iron supplements can be prescribed by your physician if necessary. The best form is ferrous iron or organic iron, and they are available in a wide variety of doses – usually up to 300mg.

LEFT *Dark chocolate should only be eaten occasionally, but it does have the benefit of providing iron.*

SPECIAL NOTES

❖ Toxicity is rare, but excess iron can cause constipation. Children are at higher risk of iron poisoning and it is recommended that you keep all supplements out of their reach.

❖ Ferric iron will destroy vitamin E.

❖ Consuming caffeine drinks with, or within an hour of, a meal can inhibit absorption of iron by up to 80 percent.

❖ Only about 8 percent of iron taken orally will actually be absorbed by the bloodstream.

❖ Copper, cobalt, manganese, and vitamin C are required for iron to be used by the body, and should be taken at the same time.

❖ Women with heavy menstrual periods will require iron supplements, as may pregnant and lactating women.

LEFT *Women lose twice as much iron as men. They are especially susceptible when pregnant or breast-feeding. Iron deficiency may lead to impaired hearing, anemia, pallor, breathlessness, and fatigue.*

Magnesium

MG

The mineral magnesium is required for virtually every biochemical process in the body, and deficiencies are fairly common. Many symptoms can signal deficiency, including a disrupted heartbeat, palpitations, poor circulation, muscle spasm and cramps, nervousness and anxiety, among others. Stress can deplete magnesium levels, as can a high consumption of tea and coffee. Magnesium supplementation is not appropriate for some people (see Special Notes opposite).

RIGHT *Magnesium deficiency in young children has been linked with hyperactive behavior.*

DATA FILE

U.K. R.N.I. *300mg*   U.S. R.D.A. *350mg*

Magnesium is a mineral that is absolutely essential for every biochemical process in our bodies, including metabolism and the synthesis of both nucleic acids and protein.

- Repairs and maintains body cells
- Necessary for hormonal activity in the body
- Required for most body processes, including energy production
- Balances and controls potassium, calcium, and sodium
- Helps to bind calcium to tooth enamel
- Antidiabetic
- Required for contraction and relaxation of muscles, including heart
- Required for transmission of nerve impulses
- Magnesium is required for growth and repair
- Necessary for bone development

Deficiency symptoms
Magnesium deficiency is very common, particularly in the elderly, heavy drinkers, pregnant women, and regular, strenuous exercisers, and it has been proved that even a very slight deficiency can cause a disruption of the heartbeat, and a huge range of deficiency symptoms and signs, which include anorexia, anemia, reduced ability to detoxify, nervousness and anxiety, palpitations, muscle spasms and cramps, facial tics, loss of bone mass and density, diabetes (late onset), insomnia, hyperactivity in children, blood pressure problems, P.M.S., poor circulation, menstrual pains, kidney stones, and others. Chronic fatigue syndrome is now thought to be related to functional magnesium deficiency, when there are adequate levels in the blood but it is not absorbed into the cells. In such cases, vitamin B6 may be necessary to help transport the magnesium across the cell membrane.

Good sources
Brown rice, soybeans, nuts, brewer's yeast, wholegrains, bitter chocolate, legumes.

Therapeutic uses
Kidney stones, asthma, osteoporosis, depression and anxiety, energy problems (including chronic fatigue), P.M.S., menstrual pains, fibromyalgia, glaucoma, diabetes, strength and endurance in athletes, hypoglycemia, insomnia, migraine, gum disease, high cholesterol, high blood pressure, eclampsia, some types of hearing loss, prostate problems.

MAGNESIUM IS
NEEDED FOR
ENERGY
PRODUCTION

MAGNESIUM IS
NEEDED TO
TRANSMIT
NERVE IMPULSES

DEFICIENCY
MAY CAUSE AN
IRREGULAR
HEARTBEAT

CRAMP MAY
BE A SIGN OF
MAGNESIUM
DEFICIENCY

ABOVE *Magnesium
deficiency is common
among those who
exercise too hard.*

SPECIAL NOTES

Magnesium is toxic to people with renal problems or atrio-ventricular blocks. Otherwise magnesium should be safe. Very rarely, symptoms of excess can occur, including flushing of the skin, low blood pressure, thirst, and shallow breathing.

❖ High consumption of coffee and tea can cause the body to excrete more magnesium, so extra may be required. The contraceptive pill, chronic diarrhea, Irritable Bowel Syndrome (I.B.S.), and the use of laxatives will also compromise magnesium levels.

❖ Stress, both emotional and physical, can deplete magnesium levels, and your requirements will increase in stressful periods of your life.

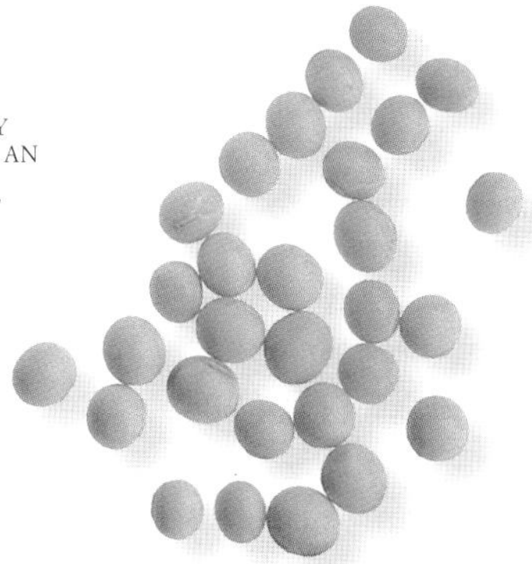

BELOW *Include plenty
of pulses (legumes) in
your diet to insure an
adequate supply of
magnesium.*

SOYBEANS

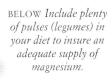

BLACK-EYED PEAS

DOSAGE

*Dietary intake is
thought to be inadequate
in the average Western diet;
supplements of 200 to 400mg are
recommended daily. Best forms
are magnesium citrate and
magnesium taurate. Good
multivitamin and mineral
supplements should have
a healthy dose
of magnesium.*

Zinc

ZN

Zinc is one of the most important trace elements, playing a part in many vital body processes, including genetic communication, and protection of the immune system. White spots on fingernails, and certain skin problems, may suggest deficiency. While mild deficiency is common, supplementation over 30mg a day can unbalance other nutrients, requiring increased copper, iron, and selenium intake.

LEFT *Mushrooms are a good source of natural zinc. Try to eat them regularly.*

POOR VISION

HEARING PROBLEMS

IMPAIRED SENSE OF SMELL

TASTE BUDS MAY NOT FUNCTION CORRECTLY

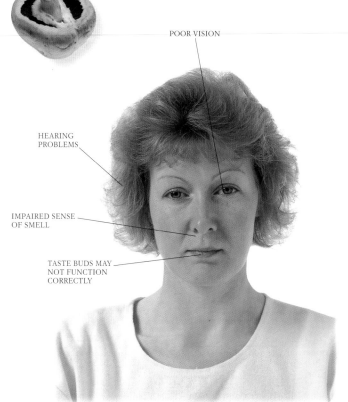

LEFT *An inadequate supply of zinc may result in malfunctions of the sensory organs.*

SPECIAL NOTES

❖ Zinc is thought to be nontoxic, although very high doses may cause some nausea, vomiting, and diarrhea.

❖ Women who are pregnant or breast-feeding will have increased zinc requirements.

❖ Chronic illness, surgery, wounds, and infections require extra zinc in order for healing to take place.

❖ Try to avoid drinking tea or coffee in the same meal as zinc-rich foods or supplements, since they can inhibit its metabolism.

❖ Zinc deficiency may also be high in those taking the contraceptive pill, or taking iron or folic acid supplements.

❖ The best forms of zinc are zinc citrate, zinc gluconate, zinc picolinate, and zinc monomethionine.

BELOW *To help prevent the effects of aging include zinc-rich foods, such as oysters, eggs, and seeds in your diet.*

DOSAGE

Take with a good multivitamin and mineral supplement. Daily, 15 to 30mg is useful; increase copper, iron, and selenium intake if taking more zinc than that.

BELOW *Zinc deficiency in pregnant women is associated with low birthweight babies.*

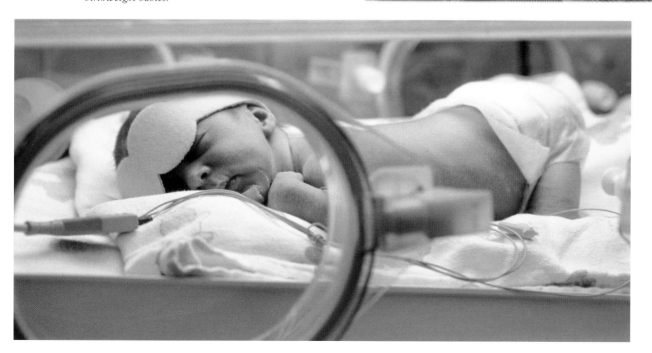

Boron

B

The importance of the trace element boron is only just being discovered. We now know that people who live in areas where the soil has a high boron content are believed to be less likely to suffer from arthritis. Very little is needed by the body, however, and deficiency symptoms are not well known.

SPECIAL NOTES

❖ Boron may be toxic in doses above about 100mg. Symptoms of toxicity include a red rash, vomiting, diarrhea, reduced circulation, shock, and then coma.

❖ It is also claimed that boron will raise testosterone levels and build muscle in men. It is therefore commonly used by budding athletes and body-builders.

DATA FILE

U.K. R.N.I. *none* **U.S. R.D.A.** *none*

Boron is a trace mineral found in most plants, and it is now believed to be an essential nutrient for health. Recent research has reported that boron added to the diets of postmenopausal women prevented calcium loss and bone demineralization. Furthermore, evidence shows that inhabitants of countries with a high boron content in the soil are less likely to suffer from arthritis.

- Helps to maintain appropriate body levels of minerals and hormones needed for bone health
- May help to reduce calcium loss in post-menopausal women
- Helps to prevent osteoporosis
- Builds muscle

Deficiency symptoms
There are no comprehensive deficiency symptoms, although bone conditions, such as osteomalacia and osteoarthritis, may result, as well as growth depression, problems metabolizing calcium, magnesium, and phosphorus, and increased effects of stress on the body.

Good sources
Pears, prunes, pulses, raisins, tomatoes, apples.

Therapeutic uses
Arthritis, osteoporosis, menopause symptoms, muscle building, external treatment of fungal and bacterial infections.

RIGHT *Apples, like pears, are an excellent source of boron and can be included easily in your daily diet.*

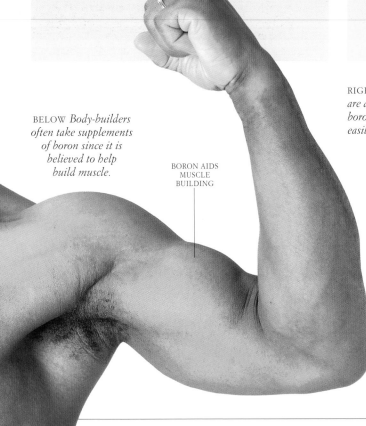

BELOW *Body-builders often take supplements of boron since it is believed to help build muscle.*

BORON AIDS
MUSCLE
BUILDING

DOSAGE

Best taken as part of a good multivitamin and mineral tablet, although it can be taken separately. Experts recommend that doses above 3mg are usually unnecessary, unless used therapeutically under the supervision of a registered practitioner.

Cobalt

CO

An inadequate intake of cobalt can contribute to anemia, because it is a constituent of vitamin B12. Deficiency, however, is rare, although more common in vegans or vegetarians. It is not often found as a supplement on its own, and excessive amounts are toxic, but it will, in tiny amounts, form part of many good multivitamin and mineral preparations.

SPINACH

ZUCCHINI

BROCCOLI

CABBAGE

LEFT *Green and leafy vegetables are a good source of cobalt if grown in cobalt-rich soil.*

BELOW *Cobalt is a constituent of vitamin B12 which is necessary for the production of red blood cells.*

Cobalt is an essential trace mineral that is a constituent of vitamin B12. The amount of cobalt you have in your body is dependent on the amount of cobalt in the soil, and therefore in the food we eat. Most of us are not deficient in cobalt, although deficiency is much more common in vegetarians. Only very small amounts of this mineral are required in the body, and its main (and some say only) function is to prevent anemia.

Works with vitamin B12 in:
- the production of red blood cells
- to insure the health of the nervous system

Deficiency symptoms
There are no specific deficiency symptoms of cobalt, but as a component of vitamin B12, anemia can result from an inadequate intake.

Good sources
Fresh leafy green vegetables, meat, liver, milk, oysters, clams.

Therapeutic uses
Used only as a part of B12 to prevent pernicious anemia, to help in the production of red blood cells, and for nervous system problems.

SPECIAL NOTE

Excessive amounts of cobalt, or its compounds, can cause nausea, damage to the heart, kidneys, and nerves, and even death.

DOSAGE

Cobalt is rarely found in supplement form, but forms part of a good multivitamin and mineral supplement with the B-complex vitamins. No daily allowance is set, but 8mcg is suggested as a necessary quantity in the diet.

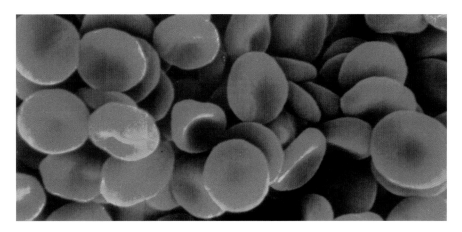

Chromium

CR

Chromium's role was discovered only a few decades ago. It is now known to help regulate blood-sugar levels and has been used to treat diabetes. Because it is used, along with magnesium and the B vitamins, to metabolize sugar, excess sugar intake can deplete stores. The mineral also controls blood-cholesterol levels.

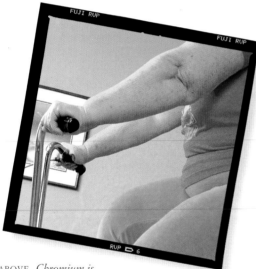

ABOVE *Chromium is useful for those who need to lose weight because it may suppress hunger pangs.*

DATA FILE

U.K. Minimum suggested intake *25mcg*
U.S. Safe adequate intake range *50–200mcg*

Chromium is a trace mineral that was discovered to be important to our health in the 1950s. It is an important regulator of blood sugar and has been used successfully in the control and treatment of diabetes. Chromium functions as the glucose-tolerance factor, or G.T.F., which stimulates insulin activity, controls blood glucose by encouraging its uptake by muscles and organs, stimulates glucose metabolism, controls blood-cholesterol levels, controls fat levels in the blood, reduces arteriosclerosis, stimulates the synthesis of proteins, increases resistance to infections, and suppresses hunger pains.

The body requires chromium, magnesium, and B vitamins in order to metabolize sugar, and a diet that has excess sugar will very quickly rob the body of these essential nutrients. There is some evidence that the Western diet, which is high in sugar and refined foods, is substantially lacking in chromium, which may be the cause of a number of common health problems.

- Chromium works in the body as the glucose-tolerance factor that stimulates insulin activity

Deficiency symptoms
Diabetes (particularly adult-onset), hypoglycemia, fatigue, mood swings, high blood cholesterol, and atherosclerosis.

Good sources
Liver, wholegrain cereals, meat, cheese, brewer's yeast, molasses, mushrooms, egg yolk.

Therapeutic uses
High cholesterol levels, hypoglycemia, diabetes, heart disease, depression and anxiety, P.M.S.-related symptoms.

SPECIAL NOTES

❖ Toxicity is rare because less than 10 percent of chromium taken in by the body is absorbed.
❖ Some people experience troubled dreams when taking chromium supplements.
❖ Should only be taken by diabetics on instruction from a physician.

❖ People who experience mood swings associated with blood-sugar drops may benefit from chromium, as will dieters, since it may help to control the appetite.

BELOW *The Western diet, which is high in sugar and processed foods, is most likely to be chromium deficient.*

DOSAGE

About 100 to 200mcg is considered to be adequate for most people, with higher doses used therapeutically. Chromium polynicotinate has the highest G.T.F. activity.

Copper

CU

Copper is a trace element, which works with iron in synthesizing hemoglobin in the red blood cells. It is an antioxidant and is also important for the production of collagen. We get most of it from copper pipes, cooking utensils, and harmful influences such as pollution and smoking, not from fresh foods. Better sources include wholegrains.

BELOW *Although most of our copper comes from non-food sources, it can also be found in shellfish.*

DOSAGE

Copper appears in many good multivitamin and mineral supplements and could be taken alone up to 3mg. Optimum daily doses are between 1 and 2mg.

DATA FILE

U.K. R.N.I. *1.2mg* **U.S. Safe adequate intake** *2–3mg*

Copper is an essential trace mineral and is necessary for the act of respiration – iron and copper are required for hemoglobin to be synthesized in the red blood cells. Copper is also important for the production of collagen, which is responsible for the health of our bones, cartilage, and skin. Copper is one of the antioxidant minerals *(see pp. 18–19)*, **which protect against free-radical damage. Our normal daily intake is between 2 and 5mg of copper, exceeding the body-maintenance requirements of about 2mg per day. Most copper is not obtained from fresh food, but from copper pipes, cooking utensils, and ironically, from unhealthy sources, such as processed food, cigarettes, birth control pills, and pollution, particularly that from automobiles.**

- Necessary for production of adrenal hormones
- Helps iron absorption
- Necessary to maintain blood vessels and connective tissues
- Necessary for the production of energy
- Antioxidant
- Maintains nerve fibers
- Essential for utilization of vitamin C
- Makes tyrosine usable, which provides skin and hair color
- Regulates cholesterol
- Inactivates histamine

Deficiency symptoms
Anemia, edema, skin pigmentation problems, hemorrhaging, hair problems, irritability, and loss of taste.

Good sources
Avocados, animal livers, molasses, wholegrains, shellfish, nuts, fruit, oysters, kidneys, legumes.

Therapeutic uses
Anemia, rheumatism, and arthritis, some cancers, energy problems.

SPECIAL NOTES

❖ Excess intake, e.g. 10mg, can cause vomiting, diarrhea, muscular pain, depression, irritability, nervousness, and dementia, but toxicity is low and very rare.

❖ Eating a good diet, rich in wholegrains and leafy green vegetables, will preclude supplementation.

❖ Like iron supplements, keep copper supplements away from children.

❖ Supplements that do not contain copper can cause a deficiency by providing nutrients that compete with copper for absorption, such as zinc. Zinc and copper should not be taken at the same time (take them some hours apart instead), unless in the form of a well-balanced multivitamin.

❖ Supplementation can lower the levels of zinc in the body and cause insomnia; however, therapeutic use of copper can be undertaken by a trained nutritionist who will take these side effects into account.

RIGHT *Copper may be absorbed through the skin from a bracelet or obtained from foods, such as avocado.*

Fluorine

F

Fluorine, or fluoride, is important for protection against tooth decay, although in excess amounts it can actually mottle the teeth. Fluoride is added to the water supply in many countries, an issue that has been hotly debated since it is found naturally in many foods. It is not recommended that you supplement fluoride, unless it is advised by your physician or dentist.

DATA FILE

U.K. R.N.I. *none* **U.S. R.D.A.** *none*

Fluorine is a trace mineral found naturally in soil, water, plants, and animal tissues. Its electrically charged form is "fluoride," which is how we usually refer to it. Although it has not yet been officially recognized as an essential nutrient, studies show that it is important in many processes and may play a major role in the prevention of many 20th-century killers, such as heart disease. The major source of fluorine is drinking water, which is normally fluoridated or else has enough naturally occurring fluoride to make fluoridation unnecessary.

- Helps to protect against dental caries
- Protects against and treats osteoporosis
- May help to prevent heart disease
- May help to prevent the calcification of organs and musculoskeletal structures

Deficiency symptoms
Tooth decay, osteoporosis; may cause infertility or anemia.

Good sources
Seafood, animal meat, black tea.

Therapeutic uses
Tooth decay, weak bones.

SPECIAL NOTES

❖ Fluoride supplements should always be taken with calcium.

❖ Do not take fluoride supplements without consulting your physician or dentist.

❖ 10 to 80mg is considered to be a toxic dose, which can cause serious tooth and bone problems, as well as overstimulation of the parathyroid glands. Slightly lower doses may cause energy problems and lead to calcification of the tendons and ligaments.

❖ In adults 0.5–2.6g per day gives rise to acute and potentially fatal fluorosis.

❖ Fluoride is also found in most foods, and there is considerable debate about whether it is necessary to fluoridate our supply of drinking water.

❖ Excess fluoride, even in small quantities, can cause mottling of the teeth, and osteoporosis and bone spurs. However, in the correct quantities, fluoride is invaluable for preventing tooth decay, and encouraging strong bones and teeth.

RIGHT *Piped water and black tea with lemon are excellent sources of fluorine.*

LEFT *Fluorine is commonly added to piped water in areas where naturally occurring levels of this mineral are insufficient.*

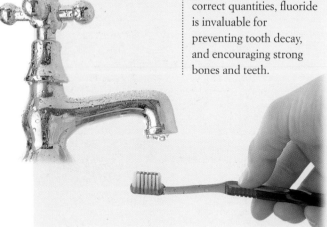

DOSAGE

Major source is drinking water, and typical daily intake is 1 to 2mg. Tablets and drops are available from pharmacies, but should be limited to 1mg daily in adults, and 0.25 to 0.5mg for children. It is not recommended that you take fluoride supplements without consulting your physician or dentist. It is not normally found in multivitamin and mineral supplements.

Iodine

I

Iodine is the Greek word for "violet," the color of this important mineral. The main function of iodine is to produce hormones in the thyroid gland, and it is found in seafood and seaweed. Goiter, which is an enlargement of the thyroid gland, is common in parts of the world where the soil lacks iodine. In these areas, iodized sea salt is recommended as a natural supplement.

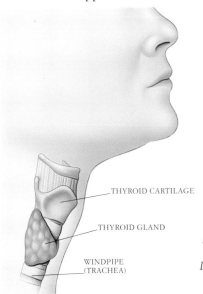

THYROID CARTILAGE

THYROID GLAND

WINDPIPE
(TRACHEA)

LEFT *Iodine is necessary for correct thyroid function. Deficiency may result in hypothyroidism or goiter.*

SPECIAL NOTES

❖ Iodine is toxic in high doses and may aggravate or cause acne. Large doses may interfere with hormone activity.

❖ Cruciferous foods such as cabbage, Brussels sprouts, cauliflower, and broccoli contain substances that can cause hypothyroidism by antagonizing iodine. But cooking will prevent this. Anyone who eats large quantities of these vegetables should consider an iodine supplement.

DATA FILE

U.K. R.N.I. *140mcg* **U.S. R.D.A.** *150mcg*

Iodine is a mineral, first discovered in 1812 in kelp. Iodine was extracted and named iodine because of its violet color. Iodine occurs naturally and is a crucial part of the thyroid hormones that regulate our energy levels. Iodine is found in seafood and seaweeds, and most table salt is fortified with iodine.

- Helps protect against toxic effects from radioactive materials
- Prevents goiter
- Produces hormones from the thyroid gland
- Promotes healthy hair, skin, nails, teeth
- Burns excess fat

Deficiency symptoms
Deficiency is very common in many parts of the world, where iodine is not found in sufficient quantities in the soil and, as a result, the incidence of goiter and cretinism is very high. Studies show that iodine deficiency is also linked to Parkinson's disease, cancer of the thyroid, multiple sclerosis, and Alzheimer's disease, among others. Deficiency symptoms include an enlarged thyroid, dry skin, neurological problems, excess estrogen production, chronic fatigue, apathy, and reduced immune activity.

Good sources
Fish and seafood, pineapple, raisins, seaweed, dairy produce.

Therapeutic uses
Cuts and wounds (as an antiseptic, used externally), goiter, fibrocystic breast disease, thyroid problems.

DOSAGE

Best taken as potassium iodide, or as seaweed products. Take under the supervision of your physician or nutritionist.

ABOVE *If you feel that you are suffering from iodine deficiency, try eating fresh pineapple.*

Potassium

K

Potassium, together with sodium and chloride, makes up the essential body salts, or electrolytes, that are crucial to the balance of fluids in the body. Potassium also plays a vital role in, for example, heartbeat, protein synthesis, and muscle contraction. It is lost in sweat, and may need replenishing after heavy exercise by eating plenty of fresh fruit or drinking vegetable juices.

ABOVE *Bananas are one of the best natural sources of potassium and should be eaten regularly.*

DOSAGE

Eat more fresh fruit and vegetables to increase potassium intake. Diuretic drugs users and those living in a hot climate may need up to 1.5g daily. Take with zinc and magnesium, as part of a good multivitamin and mineral supplement. Individuals with kidney disorders usually need to restrict their potassium intake.

DATA FILE

U.K. R.N.I. *3,500mg* **U.S. R.D.A.** *3,500mg*

Potassium is one of the most important minerals in our body, working with sodium and chloride to form "electrolytes," or essential body salts, that make up our body fluids. Potassium is crucial for body functioning, playing a role in nerve conduction, heartbeat, energy production, synthesis of nucleic acids and proteins, and muscle contraction. Sweating causes a loss of potassium, as does chronic diarrhea and use of diuretics.

• Necessary for transportation of carbon dioxide by red blood cells
• Required for water balance and protein synthesis
• Electrolyte
• Necessary for nerve and muscle function
• Stabilizes internal structure of cells
• Acts with sodium to conduct nerve impulses
• Activates enzymes that control energy production
• Prevents and treats high blood pressure

Deficiency symptoms
Vomiting, dizziness, muscle weakness and paralysis, water retention, low blood pressure, thirst, drowsiness and confusion, and overwhelming fatigue.

Good sources
Avocados, leafy green vegetables, bananas, dried fruits, fruit and vegetable juices, nuts, soy flour, potatoes, molasses.

Therapeutic uses
Not used therapeutically at present.

SPECIAL NOTES

❖ Excessive potassium may cause muscular weakness and mental apathy, eventually stopping the heart. It may also cause ulceration of the small intestine.
❖ Fresh fruits and vegetables (both of which are good sources of potassium) should be consumed on a daily basis in order to avoid deficiency.
❖ There is some evidence that potassium may help to prevent and treat cancer, and this theory forms the basis of Dr. Max Gerson's therapeutic diet, which is high in fresh fruit and vegetable juices.

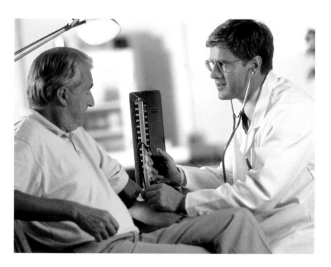

ABOVE *Potassium helps to normalize blood pressure. Supplement your diet if you suffer from hypertension.*

Manganese

MN

Manganese plays an important part in normal brain functioning. It is now believed to be an antioxidant, although research into this important trace element is in its infancy. Manganese plays many important roles in the body, including the maintenance of healthy brain function, and toxicity is very rare.

SPECIAL NOTES

❖ Toxicity is very rare, but may include lethargy, involuntary movements, posture problems, and eventually coma. Manganese is, however, one of the least toxic of the trace minerals because it is excreted readily by the body. Environmental toxicity may be possible.

❖ Absorption is less efficient when accompanied by calcium, iron, and phytate (which is found in bran).

RIGHT *Manganese supplements may be used therapeutically for sufferers of Alzheimer's disease.*

DATA FILE

U.K. R.N.I. *None, but estimate lowest acceptable intake is 1.4mg*
U.S. R.D.A. *none, but range of acceptable intake is 2.5–5mg*

Manganese is an essential trace element that is necessary for the normal functioning of the brain, and it is effective in the treatment of numerous nervous disorders, including Alzheimer's disease and schizophrenia. Our understanding of manganese is still incomplete, but it may prove to be one of the most important nutrients in human pathology. It is likely that manganese is one of the antioxidant minerals (*see pp. 18–19*)**.**

• Necessary for the functioning of the brain
• Used in the treatment of some nervous disorders
• Necessary for antioxidant activity
• Required for the metabolism of energy
• Involved in the metabolism of calcium
• Required to produce melanin and to synthesize fatty acids
• Helps to produce urea
• Necessary for building proteins and nucleic acids
• Necessary for normal bone structure
• Plays an important role in forming thyroxin, in the thyroid gland

Deficiency symptoms: **Dermatitis, problems metabolizing carbohydrates, poor memory, nervous irritability, ataxia, fatigue, blood-sugar problems, some types of schizophrenia, heavy menstrual periods, lowered threshold for fits in epileptics, fragile bones, and joint degeneration. Manganese is easily excreted from the body, so daily supplements are necessary.**

Good sources: **Cereals, tea, green leaf vegetables, whole wheat bread, pulses, liver, root vegetables, nuts.**

Therapeutic uses: **Epilepsy, Alzheimer's disease, schizophrenia, myasthenia gravis, anemia, diabetes, heart disease, athero-sclerosis, arthritis.**

DOSAGE

Best taken in a good multivitamin and mineral supplement. Doses of 2 to 5mg are considered adequate, but up to 10mg is thought to be safe.

Molybdenum

MO

Molybdenum is an essential trace element, although its qualities are still poorly understood. It is believed to be an antioxidant, to protect against cancer, and to help prevent anemia. Molybdenum is toxic in doses above 10mg, and although no recommended daily dose has been provided, it forms a useful part of many multivitamin and mineral preparations.

BELOW *Although molybdemum is not used therapeutically at present, it is believed to help guard against sexual impotence.*

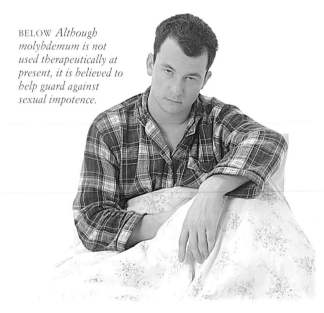

DATA FILE

U.K. R.N.I. *none, but estimated range of intake is 50–400mcg*
U.S. R.D.A. *none, but estimated range of intake is 150–500mcg*

Molybdenum is an essential trace element and a vital part of the enzyme that is responsible for the utilization of iron in our bodies. Molybdenum may also be an antioxidant, and recent research indicates that it is necessary for optimum health. In metabolism, molybdenum is a trace element that is involved in protein synthesis and oxidation reactions. Molybdenum can help to prevent anemia, sexual impotence in men, and is known to promote a feeling of well-being.

- Aids in the metabolism of fats and carbohydrates
- Vital for the utilization of iron
- Protects against cancer
- Prevents anemia because it is necessary for iron metabolism
- Necessary for the production of uric acid
- Necessary for synthesis of taurine
- Helps to prevent sexual impotence in men
- Helps to protect against dental caries

- Necessary for D.N.A. metabolism

Deficiency symptoms
Irregular heartbeat, irritability, inability to produce uric acid.

Good sources
Buckwheat, canned beans, wheatgerm, liver, pulses, wholegrains, offal, eggs.

Therapeutic uses
Not used therapeutically at present.

SPECIAL NOTES

❖ Molybdenum is toxic in doses higher than 10 to 15mg, which cause goutlike symptoms.
❖ A high intake of copper or sulfate (that is, ferrous sulfate iron supplements) can decrease absorption of molybdenum by the body.

BELOW *All types of canned beans are known to be an excellent source of the element molybdenum.*

DOSAGE

Experts suggest 50 to 100mcg per day as a preventive measure, and it is advised that you take it as part of a good multivitamin and mineral tablet.

RIGHT *Foods rich in molybdenum include eggs and wholegrain bread.*

Phosphorus

P

One of the functions of phosphorus is to help create the structure of the bones. Although it is an important mineral, it is also widespread, so deficiency is rare. It is, however, crucial that calcium and phosphorus are balanced. Phosphorus is commonly found in soft drinks and "fast foods," so a poor diet can result in an extremely high intake, leading to a calcium imbalance.

RIGHT *Phosphorus is present in many soft drinks. Too high an intake may result in calcium imbalance.*

DATA FILE

U.K. R.N.I. *550mg* U.S. R.D.A. *800mg*

Phosphorus is a mineral that is essential to the structure and function of the body. It is present in the body as phosphates, and in this form aids the process of bone mineralization and helps to create the structure of the bones. Phosphorus is also essential for communication between cells, and for energy production.

- Forms bones, teeth, and cell membranes
- Burns sugar for energy
- Acts as a cofactor for many enzymes and activates B-complex vitamins
- Increases endurance
- Forms R.N.A. and D.N.A.

Deficiency symptoms
Phosphorus appears in many foods – including soft drinks and a number of food additives – and deficiency is rare. Some chronic conditions can, however, lead to low levels of phosphorus in the body, and symptoms of this type of deficiency include debility, mental confusion, weakness, loss of appetite, irritability, speech problems, anemia, lowered resistance to infection, and osteomalacia.

Good sources
Meat, fish, yeast, wholegrains, cheese, soy products, nuts.

Therapeutic uses
Phosphorus is used therapeutically for conditions listed above that are caused or exacerbated by a disease-related phosphorous deficiency.

ABOVE *Phosphorus increases endurance, and boosts energy levels in those in a weakened state.*

SPECIAL NOTES

❖ Toxicity may occur with dosages or intake above 1g per day, and may cause diarrhea, calcification of organs and soft tissues, and prevent the absorption of iron, zinc, calcium, and magnesium.
❖ Studies show that long-term imbalance between calcium and phosphorus can cause osteoporosis.

When phosphorus intake is too high (often from too many soft drinks or other fast-food items that are so common in the Western diet), the parathyroid hormone secretion is stimulated, which causes phosphorus to be excreted from the body and calcium to be mobilized.

DOSAGE

Phosphorus deficiency usually accompanies deficiency in potassium, magnesium, and zinc, so insure a good multivitamin and mineral supplement has all four. Adequate amounts are usually found in the diet; supplementation of phosphorus on its own should only be undertaken with supervision.

Selenium

SE

Selenium is one of the most talked-about trace elements of the moment. It has recently been discovered to be an antioxidant, and to provide protection against many cancers, as well as age-related conditions. Studies show that it may even help in the treatment of A.I.D.S. Our requirements are low, but deficiency is common where the soil is deficient for example, in the U.K.

DOSAGE

Dosages of 400 to 1,000mcg have been used for immune stimulation, and for anticarcinogenic effects, but 50 to 200mcg should be adequate to experience benefits. The best form of supplementation is selenium-rich yeast, and L-selenomethionine. Take with 30 to 400iu of vitamin E for best effect.

ABOVE *Onions provide rich sources of selenium and may help protect against cancer and heart disease.*

SPECIAL NOTES

❖ Toxic in small doses; beware of blackened fingernails or garlic odor on skin and breath.
❖ Diets that are high in refined foods are more likely selenium deficient.
❖ Cereals are dependent upon the amount of selenium in the soil for their selenium content, and countries with low soil-selenium levels include the U.K., Finland, and other parts of Europe, New Zealand, and China. Experts recommend that you try to eat breads baked with grains from countries such as Canada, where the soil is selenium rich. If you cannot do so, take a supplement daily.

DATA FILE

U.K. R.N.I. *75mcg* **U.S. R.D.A.** *70mcg*

Selenium is an essential trace element that has recently been recognized as one of the most important nutrients in our diet. It is an antioxidant (*see pp. 18–19*) and is vitally important in human metabolism. Selenium has been proved to provide protection against a number of cancers, and other diseases. Studies have shown that selenium can help protect against such age-related diseases as heart disease, cancer, and arthritis, and may also be beneficial in the treatment and prevention of immune-deficient conditions, including H.I.V. and A.I.D.S. The body requires only tiny amounts of selenium each day, but it is essential, particularly for its role in protecting the cell membranes and improving their overall function.

- Antioxidant
- Necessary for the repair of D.N.A.
- Required for a healthy immune system
- Prevents many cancers
- Improves liver function
- Maintains healthy eyes and eyesight
- Maintains healthy skin and hair
- Protects against heart and circulatory diseases
- May impede the aging process
- Can detoxify alcohol, many drugs, smoke, and some fats
- Increases male potency and sex drive

Deficiency symptoms
Cataracts, impaired growth, heart disease, reduced immunity and resistance to infections, inflammation of the muscles, reduced fertility in men, age spots, cancerous changes, and reduced ability to detoxify.

Good sources
Wheatgerm, wheatbran, tuna fish, onions, whole-wheat bread, tomatoes, broccoli.

Therapeutic uses
Dandruff, cancers, acne, arthritis, asthma, sperm motility, thyroid function, kidney problems, A.I.D.S., muscular dystrophy, hepatitis, epilepsy.

BELOW *Tuna fish is a good source of selenium. Include it in your diet to boost the immune system.*

ABOVE *Selenium is believed to offer protection against a number of cancers.*

Vanadium

V

Vanadium is another trace element only recently proven to be necessary for human life (see also Selenium). It may even offer a clue to the causes of manic depression, which may be linked, not to a deficiency, but to a surfeit of the mineral. In the right amounts, it is important to the process that balances sodium and potassium in the body.

DATA FILE

U.K. R.N.I. *none* U.S. R.D.A. *none*

Vanadium is a trace mineral that has only recently proved necessary for human life. At the turn of the century, French physicians believed that vanadium was a miracle cure for a variety of illnesses, but it proved to be toxic at the levels they were prescribing, and so became less popular. Today, it is believed that elevated levels of vanadium may cause manic depression, which is perhaps a clue to a little-understood disease. It appears to be involved in bone mineralization and has insulin-like qualities. Vanadium may also inhibit the activity of the sodium pump, which balances the amounts of sodium and potassium in the body.

- May slow down the formation of cholesterol in the blood vessels
- May prevent heart disease and heart attacks
- May help to prevent dental caries
- May help to reduce high blood pressure
- May reduce blood sugar

Deficiency symptoms
None known.

Good sources
Parsley, radishes, gelatin, lettuce, lobster, bonemeal.

Therapeutic uses
Diabetes (experimentally).

DOSAGE

Supplements are not available, although some of the newer multivitamin and mineral supplements may contain low levels of this element.

RIGHT *Vanadium was prescribed by early 20th-century French physicians, but in doses that were toxic.*

ABOVE *Increase your natural intake of vanadium by including radishes in your diet.*

SPECIAL NOTES

❖ Vanadium is very toxic and is linked to manic depression in high quantities.
❖ High levels of vitamin C are said to reduce vanadium levels present in the body.

❖ Vanadium antagonizes chromium and may cause deficiency (*see p. 56*) when taken in excess. Foods with a low-chromium, high-vanadium content include skim milk, fish, seaweed, and intensively farmed chickens.

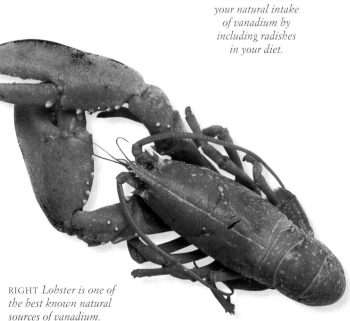

RIGHT *Lobster is one of the best known natural sources of vanadium.*

Amino acids

Amino acids are organic compounds that comprise the "building blocks" of protein. They are necessary to make just about all the constituents of the body, from hair and skin to blood. We get them from the proteins in food, and of the many that have been identified, around 14 are reasonably well understood: these are covered in the following pages. Amino acids should not be supplemented without medical supervision.

A number of amino acids play an essential role in our bodies. Many different amino acids are found, about 20 of which are the main constituents of proteins; only about half of these are classified as essential nutrients – that is, necessary in the human diet.

Proteins are an indispensable substance in our diets because of their constituent amino acids. Nutritionally, complete proteins are those that contain the right concentrations of the amino acids that humans cannot synthesize from other amino acids or other sources. An adequate intake, however, may be achieved by consuming a correct mixture of proteins, some of which might be deficient in one amino acid but rich in another.

Some of the amino acids are used directly as building blocks in the synthesis of new proteins, while others may be used to supply energy, and still others, particularly when large amounts of proteins are consumed, may be excreted in the urine.

Amino acids are necessary to make almost all elements in the body, including hair, skin, bone, other body tissues, antibodies, hormones, enzymes, and blood. Experts suggest that they should not be supplemented without the supervision of a trained practitioner.

L-ARGININE

- Boosts immunity
- Fights cancer by inhibiting the growth of a number of tumors
- Helps build muscle and burns fat, by stimulating the pituitary glands to increase the secretion of the growth hormone
- Helps heal burns and other wounds
- Helps protect the liver and detoxify harmful substances
- Increases sperm count in men with a low count
- L-arginine is one of the most important and most useful amino acids, with a significant role in muscle growth and healing, helping to regulate and support key components of the immune system
- It is also very important for male fertility
- L-arginine is a non-essential amino acid, which means that it is capable of being synthesized in the body and it is, therefore, not essential that we get additional amounts in our daily diet; it is, however, essential for children
- Arginine with lysine can inhibit herpes attacks in carriers; arginine alone should not be taken by anyone with herpes simplex infections
- Best sources are raw cereals, chocolate, nuts
- The optimal intake is unknown, but supplemental doses up to 1.5g appear to be safe

BRAZIL NUTS

ABOVE AND RIGHT *Nuts and cereals are a rich source of L-arginine and may help boost the immune system.*

CORNFLAKES

CAUTION

Take L-arginine on an empty stomach, and do not take in excess since it could cause mental and metabolic disturbances, nausea, and diarrhea. It should not be taken by anyone with a history of schizophrenia. Prolonged high doses may be dangerous.

L-ASPARTIC ACID

- Disposes of ammonia, helping to protect the central nervous system
- Helps treat fatigue
- May improve stamina and endurance
- L-aspartic acid is classified as a non-essential amino acid and has been used for many years in the treatment of chronic fatigue; studies confirm the efficiency of this amino acid in raising energy levels, and in helping to overcome the side effects of drug withdrawal

- Supplements are available in 250 to 500mg tablets; if advised by a physician or nutritionist, take three times daily with juice or water
- May cause flatulence

CAUTION

Do not take with proteins, such as milk. Do not take more than 1g without the supervision of your physician.

ASPARTIC ACID
SUPPLEMENT

L-CYSTEINE

- May protect against copper toxicity
- Protects the body against free radicals (*see pp. 18–19*)
- May help to reverse damage done by smoking and alcohol abuse
- Offers protection against nuclear radiation and X-rays
- May help arthritis
- Helps to repair D.N.A. and therefore prevent the effects of aging
- L-cysteine contains sulfur, which is said to work as an antioxidant, protecting and preserving the cells in our body
- Best sources are eggs, meat, dairy products, and some cereals

- It is also said to protect the body against pollutants, but much work has still to be done to understand the effects of this amino acid
- Take with vitamin C for best effect (three times as much vitamin C as L-cysteine); doses up to 1g are considered to be safe, but it is best to consult your physician first
- A non-essential amino acid
- Not recommended for pregnant or lactating women

L-GLUTAMINE

- May help to speed the healing of peptic ulcers
- May help to counter depression
- May help to energize the mind
- May help to treat and prevent colitis
- L-glutamine is a derivative of glutamic acid, which is believed to help reduce cravings for alcohol
- Studies are inconclusive

as to the real benefits of taking this amino acid, and it is not recommended that you take more than 1g daily; up to 1g daily is believed to be safe, but none-the-less take it only with the supervision of your physician
- A non-essential amino acid, not thus far found in food

ABOVE *The amino acid L-cysteine offers some protection against the harmful effects of X-rays.*

CAUTION

Diabetics should not take L-cysteine supplements unless supervised by their physician. L-cysteine may also cause kidney stones, but a high vitamin C intake should prevent this from occurring.

GLYCINE

- May help to treat low pituitary-gland function
- May be used in the treatment of spastic movement – particularly in patients suffering from multiple sclerosis
- May help to treat progressive muscular dystrophy
- Used in the treatment of hypoglycemia, since it stimulates the release of glucagon, which mobilizes glycogen that can then be released into the bloodstream as glucose

- Glycine is the simplest of the amino acids, with a variety of properties that are still being studied. It is non-essential
- It is not recommended that you take this amino acid as a supplement unless supervised by your physician; doses below 1g are thought to be safe, but research is ongoing
- Gelatin contains glycine

ABOVE *Glycine may be used to treat patients with spastic movements, including those with M.S.*

L-CARNITINE

- Regulates the metabolism of fat
- Helps to break down branched-chain amino acids
- Controls ketone levels in the blood
- L-carnitine is classified as a non-essential amino acid, but it is required for many functions
- Its most important function is its role in regulating fat metabolism – in other words, transporting fat across membranes to the energy-burning parts of cells; the more carnitine available, the faster the fat is transported, and the more fat used for energy
- Recent studies show that carnitine may be useful in the treatment of some forms of heart disease and in muscular dystrophy

- Food sources of carnitine include meats and dairy foods
- Supplementation is believed to be safe between 1.5 and 2g daily, although experts recommend that you take it for no more than one week a month; 500mg daily is thought to be adequate dosage for improving athletic performance
- Some gastrointestinal side effects
- Not to be taken by pregnant or lactating women or people with kidney damage

L-CARNITINE REGULATES FAT METABOLISM

RIGHT *L-carnitine helps transport fat to the energy burning parts of cells, so that the fat may be used for energy.*

L-CARNITINE MAY HELP PREVENT HEART DISEASE

CONTROLS KETONE LEVELS IN THE BLOOD

L-HISTIDINE

- Used in the treatment of arthritis, whose sufferers have an abnormally low level of this amino acid in their blood
- Essential for infants and conditionally essential for children and adults
- L-histidine is one of the lesser known amino acids, found in many animal proteins, tofu, and seeds,

and its role in our bodies is not yet fully understood
- Do not take more than 1.5g daily unless supervised by your physician
- Always take with vitamin C. Manic depressives or schizophrenics should not take it. Not to be taken by women with heavy menstrual bleeding or pregnant/lactating women.

L-LYSINE

- Inhibits herpes – high doses are now believed to be effective in reducing the recurrence of outbreaks
- May help to build muscle mass
- Helps to prevent fertility problems
- Improves concentration
- L-lysine is an essential amino acid; it is needed for growth, tissue repair, and for the production of antibodies, hormones, and enzymes
- It should be obtained from the diet, although supplements are available
- Best sources are fish, milk, lima beans, meat, cheese, yeast, eggs; all proteins are good sources
- Up to 500mg daily is believed to be safe, although some experts recommend 1g daily at mealtimes

CAUTION

Not suitable for children, or pregnant or lactating women.

BELOW *Fish is a good source of both L-lysine and L-methionine amino acids.*

ABOVE *High doses of L-lysine are thought to help prohibit the outbreak of the herpes virus among sufferers.*

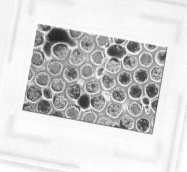

L-METHIONINE

- May help to eliminate fatty substances in the blood
- May help to regulate the nervous system
- In conjunction with choline and folic acid, it may prevent some tumors
- Necessary for the biosynthesis of taurine and cysteine
- L-methionine is a sulfur-containing essential amino acid that is very important in numerous processes in the body. Research shows that it may help to prevent clogging of the arteries by eliminating fatty substances.
- Best sources are eggs, milk, liver, and fish. Supplementation is not advised, although some physicians may suggest its use in specific circumstances.

RIGHT *Boost your intake of L-methionine naturally by adding eggs to your diet.*

L-PHENYLALANINE

- May help to alleviate depression
- May help to control addictive behavior
- Encourages mental alertness
- Promotes sexual arousal
- Reduces hunger and cravings for food
- L-phenylalanine is an essential amino acid that is necessary for a number of biochemical processes, including the synthesis of neurotransmitters present in the brain
- It is said to promote sexual arousal and to release hormones that help to control appetite
- Best sources are soy, proteins, cheese, almonds, peanuts, and sesame seeds
- L-phenylalanine is usually available in 500mg doses. Take on an empty stomach, and do not take with protein.

CAUTION

Do not take if you suffer from skin cancer or phenylketonuria. People with high blood pressure should only take it with their physician's supervision. Pregnant or lactating women should not take this amino acid. Not suitable for use with M.A.O.I. antidepressants.

DL-PHENYLALANINE

- A natural painkiller, useful for chronic pain and conditions such as migraine, neuralgia, and leg cramps
- Antidepressant
- D.L.P.A. is a form of the amino acid phenylalanine created from equal parts of D (synthetic) phenylalanine and L (natural) phenylalanine
- It has a unique role of activating and producing the endorphins in the body, which are the body's natural painkillers; many people who do not respond to conventional painkillers do respond to D.L.P.A., and its action increases over time
- Do not confuse it with L-phenylalanine

- Tablets are generally available in 375mg doses, and can be taken up to six times daily (a maximum dose of 1.5g); higher doses should only be taken under the supervision of your physician; take two to three times daily, before your meal

CAUTION

Not suitable during pregnancy, for people with phenylketonuria (P.K.U.), or those taking M.A.O.I. antidepressants. It may raise blood pressure, so check with your physician if you suffer from a circulatory disorder.

BELOW *Taurine is found only in animal products, including fish and meat.*

TAURINE

- Mild antioxidant
- Works with zinc to protect against cataracts
- Regulates nerves and muscles, and electrical activity
- Taurine is classified as a "non-essential" amino acid; it is manufactured in the body, and its main role is to regulate the nerves and muscle, and help to coordinate neuro-transmission
- Studies performed on animals show that a diet low in taurine can cause retina degeneration and impaired vision

- Excessive intake can cause depression, and other symptoms
- Doses of up to 3g are used to treat high blood pressure, epilepsy, and other conditions relating to the eyes
- Taurine is found in meat, fish, and eggs, but none of the plant foods
- 50 to 100mg is usually prescribed, taken two to three times a week
- Not recommended for pregnant or lactating women

D.L.P.A. MAY BE USED TO TREAT MIGRAINE

LEFT *DL-phenylalanine is a natural painkiller and can be used to treat both headaches and migraines.*

L-TRYPTOPHAN

- May help to encourage sleep and to prevent jet lag
- Reduces sensitivity to pain
- Reduces cravings for alcohol
- Natural antidepressant, and may help to reduce anxiety and panic attacks
- This essential amino acid is used by the brain, along with several vitamins and minerals, to produce serotonin, a neuro-transmitter present in the brain
- It was one of the first amino acids to be produced for sale as a supplement

- It is useful as a natural sleeping aid
- Used to prevent panic attacks and depression, it should be taken between meals with juice or water (no proteins)
- Best sources include cottage cheese, milk, meat, fish, turkey, bananas; proteins are generally good sources
- To help induce sleep, a physician may prescribe 500mg along with vitamin B6, niacinamide, and magnesium, to be taken an hour or so before bedtime

BELOW *Take both L-tryptophan and L-tyrosine with juice or water, not with milk.*

CAUTION

Although studies vary, it is now believed that L-tryptophan can be toxic in very high doses; there is some evidence that it may cause liver problems at high levels and may aggravate asthma and lupus. Take only on the advice of your physician. Not to be taken if on M.A.O.I. antidepressants, or by those who are pregnant or anticipating pregnancy.

L-TYROSINE

- Helps to relieve stress, encourage alertness and reduce physical symptoms of tension
- May act as an anti-depressant
- May be used to treat the emotional symptoms of P.M.S.
- May help to treat addiction to, and withdrawal from, cocaine and other drugs
- L-tyrosine is not an essential amino acid, which means that it is synthesized in the body

- Tyrosine is involved with important neurotransmitters in the brain, and it is said to energize and help to relieve the effects of stress
- Is a precursor of thyroid hormones
- Take with juice or water on an empty stomach (do not take with proteins, such as milk); some experts suggest that it is more effective when taken in conjunction with up to 25mg of vitamin B6

CAUTION

Do not take tyrosine if you suffer from migraine headaches, or if you take M.A.O.I. antidepressants. People suffering from high blood pressure or skin cancer should not take supplementary tyrosine without the approval of their physician. Not recommended for pregnant or lactating women.

ABOVE *If you wish to increase your intake of L-tryptophan naturally, try eating cottage cheese.*

Algae

Algae are plants that grow in water. Spirulina is a tiny water plant, probably the most important, in health terms, of all the algae. High in protein, with a wide range of other nutrients, it is particularly valued by vegetarians. For the Aztecs, it was a staple food. Seaweed is algae too, and it is thought to have many qualities, including an ability to protect against cancer.

LEFT AND BELOW RIGHT *Seaweeds have been used medicinally for thousands of years. They are rich in iodine.*

SEA LETTUCE

DATA FILE

- **Rich in nutrients and high in protein (particularly useful for vegetarians)**
- **May help to suppress the appetite**
- **Used to maintain skin health and to treat skin disorders**
- **May contribute to the health of the intestines**
- **General tonic properties**
- **Many have anticancer properties**

• Spirulina are blue-green bacteria or algae, which are rich in gamma linolenic acid (*see pp. 80–81*), as well as a wide variety of nutrients, including beta-carotene.
• Spirulina was used as a staple food by the Aztecs of Mexico and is now marketed as a high-protein food supplement.
• Recently, there have been a number of cases of algae contamination because some algae are grown outdoors in open lakes. Some symptoms of contamination have included hair loss. Deep-sea algae products are believed less likely to be contaminated, and are therefore safer.
• Seaweeds are another form of "algae," and there are four main types.
• Seaweeds appear in many foods, medicines, and cosmetics, and have been used therapeutically for thousands of years.
• Seaweeds are rich in iodine and are used worldwide in the treatment of goiter. They are believed to have antiviral activity, and some studies have concluded that they act as a preventive for cancer.
• Seaweeds may help to reduce the effects of carcinogenics, including radioactive material, and are therefore useful for reducing the damage done by chemotherapy and radiotherapy.
• Seaweeds are believed to be natural antacids, and are used in the treatment of intestinal disorders.

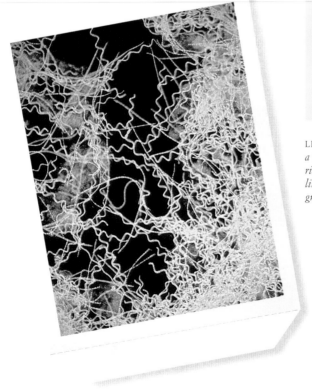

LEFT *Spirulina is a blue-green algae, rich in gamma-linolenic acid. It grows in the water.*

DULSE

Coenzyme Q10

Coenzyme Q10 is sometimes known as vitamin Q. It is a vitamin-like substance, found in many foods and existing in every cell of the body, with concentrations in the liver and heart. It plays a part in cell function and is believed to help in the treatment of obesity, diabetes, and Alzheimer's disease.

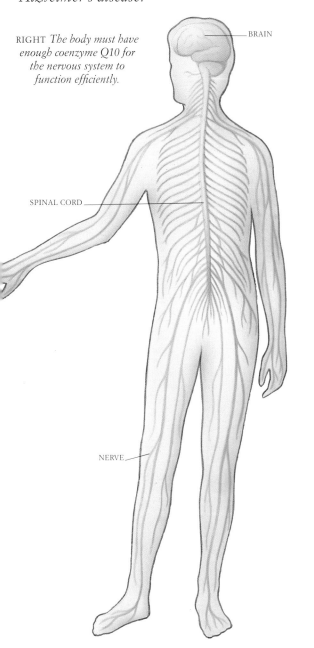

RIGHT *The body must have enough coenzyme Q10 for the nervous system to function efficiently.*

BRAIN

SPINAL CORD

NERVE

DATA FILE

- **Enhances immunity**
- **Improves the heart-muscle metabolism**
- **May prevent coronary insufficiency and heart failure**
- **Antiaging**
- **Necessary for healthy functioning of the nervous system and the brain cells**
- **Boosts energy levels**
- **Used in the treatment of gum disease**

• Coenzyme Q10 is a vitamin-like substance found in all cells of the body. It is biologically important since it forms part of the system across which electrons flow in the cells in the process of energy production. When it is deficient, the cell cannot function effectively and the rate at which the muscle cells work is adversely affected.

• Coenzyme Q10 is also known as ubiquinone or vitamin Q, and it is concentrated in the body in certain organs, especially the liver and the heart.

• Coenzyme Q10 stimulates both the immune system and overall immunity, and may help in the treatment of obesity, diabetes, and Alzheimer's disease.

• Coenzyme Q10 is found in organ meats, spinach, polyunsaturated vegetable oils, and fish such as tuna and sardines. There is no R.D.A. for coenzyme Q10, but experts recommend that 15 to 30mg, taken daily, is the optimum level for good health.

BELOW *Coenzyme Q10 occurs naturally in fish such as tuna. It boosts the immune system.*

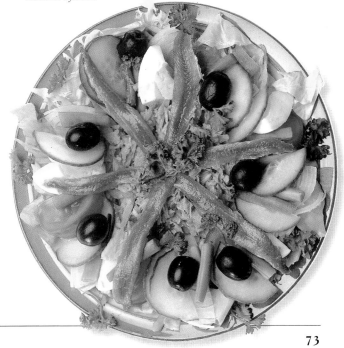

Bee Products

Three products of the bee's activities – besides the obvious one, honey – are thought to be beneficial to human health: pollen, taken by the bee into the hive; propolis, a gummy substance taken from plants and used to seal the hive; and royal jelly, produced by the worker bees as food for the queen. Those who are allergic to bee stings need to exercise caution.

ABOVE *Bee pollen, royal jelly, and propolis are all produced by the activities of the worker honey bees.*

BELOW *Bee pollen, which is found in the hive itself, forms the basic diet of all worker bees.*

BEE AND FLOWER POLLEN

- Rich in both amino acids and protein
- Help to suppress appetite and cravings
- May help to improve skin problems, and retard the aging process
- May help to treat prostate problems
- Energize the body
- Regulate the bowels
- May help to boost immunity and diminish allergies

• In flowering plants the pollen-producing spores are located in the stamens of flowers. Flower pollen is said to be purer than bee pollen. Bee pollen is found in the hives themselves. It is rich in protein and amino acids and forms, with honey, the basic diet of all the bees in the hive, except for the queen (*see Royal Jelly*).

• Pollen has been used as medicine around the world for centuries.

• Unpasteurized honey contains small amounts of bee pollen. Doses of 400mg taken daily appear to be safe levels. Always take pollen with food.

CAUTION

If you suffer from hay fever or an allergy to bee stings, you may have a reaction to bee and flower pollen. See your physician or practitioner before taking this supplement.

BELOW *Unpasteurized honey contains a small amount of bee pollen. It is one of nature's most healing foods.*

LEFT *Royal jelly, which has yeast-inhibiting properties, may prevent athelete's foot.*

PROPOLIS

- Enhances immunity
- Helps wounds to heal
- Boosts energy
- Reduces cholesterol in the blood
- Helps to reduce the incidence of colds
- Natural antibiotic

• Propolis is a sticky material collected by bees from buds or tree bark and used to seal the inside of the hive. It is a mixture of wax, resin, balsam oil, and pollen. It is said to act as an antibiotic and bactericide, and may be used to help wounds to heal. It is rich in bioflavonoids.
• Propolis is available in tablet and liquid form, and does not appear to have any toxic levels. See your practitioner for details of suitable dosage.

BELOW *The pollen-producing spores of a flowering plant can be found in the stamens of the flower.*

ROYAL JELLY

- Antibacterial
- May prevent the development of leukemia
- Yeast-inhibiting function, preventing conditions such as thrush and athlete's foot
- Contains hormone-like substances which may act like testosterone (the male hormone) to increase libido
- Used in the treatment of subfertility
- May be useful in the treatment of M.E. (myalgic encephalomyelitis) and M.D. (muscular dystrophy)
- Helps to reduce allergies
- Boosts the body's resistance to harmful side effects of chemotherapy and radiotherapy
- Controls blood-cholesterol levels

- Boosts the immune system
- Used in the treatment of skin problems, including eczema and acne
- Combined with pantothenic acid, it provides relief from the symptoms of arthritis

• Royal jelly has been used for thousands of years for its health-giving and rejuvenating properties, and it is rich in vitamins, amino acids, and minerals.
• It is also the prime source of fatty acid, which is said both to increase alertness and act as a natural tranquilizer.
• Royal jelly is secreted in the salivary glands of the worker bees to feed and stimulate the growth of the queen bee.
• Most tablets contain between 100 and 500mg of royal jelly. Optimum dosage is about 150mg per day. Fresh is better, although more expensive.

ROYAL JELLY SUPPLEMENT

CAUTION

Because this product contains pollen, it may cause a reaction in individuals who suffer from hay fever or an allergy to bee stings. See your physician or practitioner before taking this supplement.

RIGHT *Propolis has both antibiotic and bactericidal properties and is a good remedy for wounds.*

Live Bacteria

*There are certain types of "healthy" bacteria – * lactobacilli *– that work to balance the acidity and alkalinity (the pH balance) of the intestine, and insure the right balance of intestinal micro-organisms, or flora. They can also help to promote a healthy balance of micro-organisms in the vagina.*

The most common types of live beneficial bacteria are Lactobacillus acidophilus *and* Bifidobacteria bifidum, *commonly known as* acidophilus *and* bifidus. *A term has been developed to distinguish beneficial bacteria from the harmful organisms that are targeted by antibiotics: products such as* acidophilus *and* bifidus *are now referred to as "probiotics."*

All live-bacteria products are nontoxic and safe. To maintain a healthy gastrointestinal tract, take daily supplements that contain two to three billion viable organisms.

RIGHT *Live yogurt is the best source of* acidophilus. *It is both safe and beneficial for children.*

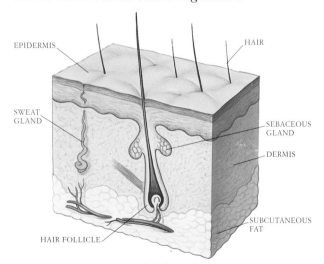

EPIDERMIS

HAIR

SWEAT GLAND

SEBACEOUS GLAND

DERMIS

SUBCUTANEOUS FAT

HAIR FOLLICLE

ABOVE *A daily supplement of* acidophilus *can help to keep your skin in good condition and prevent acne.*

ACIDOPHILUS

- **Keeps the intestines clean**
- **Prevents yeast infections of the vagina**
- **Aids the absorption of nutrients in food**
- **Can eliminate bad breath (caused by intestinal putrefaction)**
- **Can relieve and prevent constipation and flatulence**
- **Can aid in the treatment of acne and other skin problems**
- **Maintains intestinal health**

• *Acidophilus* is a source of friendly intestinal bacteria (flora). Healthy bacteria play an important role in our bodies, and unless they are continually supplied with some form of lactic acid or lactose (such as *acidophilus*) they can die, causing a host of health problems. Many physicians and health practitioners recommend taking *acidophilus* alongside oral antibiotics, which can cause diarrhea, destroy the healthy flora of the intestines, and lead to fungal infections. *Acidophilus* may also help to insure vaginal health.

• The best source is natural, unflavored, "live" yogurt, and it is also available in chewable, vanilla-flavored tablets. Keep the tablets in the refrigerator. *Acidophilus* is not toxic, is safe for children, and can be taken, with food, in unlimited amounts. Many practitioners recommend taking it as a daily supplement.

LEFT *Our bodies need healthy bacteria, or flora, in the intestines. Stores can be depleted after a course of antibiotics.*

BELOW Acidophilus *is available in chewy vanilla-flavored tablets. These pills should be kept in a refrigerator.*

BIFIDUS

- **Reduces blood-cholesterol levels**
- **Necessary for synthesizing B vitamins**
- **Inhibits harmful organisms in the body**
- **Maintains intestinal health**

- Products sold as *acidophilus* may also contain *bifidus*, and other strains of healthy bacteria. *Bifidus* works with other healthy bacteria to maintain a healthy intestinal environment.
- *Bifidobacteria* are found in human breast milk, and within a few days they establish themselves in the gut of the newborn.

Unlike *acidophilus,* which is commonly found in food, *bifidobacteria* are more difficult to obtain in large numbers through the diet. They are the most prominent helpful bacteria of the large intestine. When they are properly balanced with other helpful bacteria, they help to inhibit harmful organisms, reduce blood-cholesterol levels, and create the environment necessary for synthesizing B vitamins.

RIGHT *Babies that are breast-fed will obtain* bifidobacteria *from their mother's milk.*

77

Echinacea

The herb Echinacea has, in many circles, been hailed as the "wonder remedy" of the 1990s. Studies show that it can boost immunity, preventing infection, and help to reduce the duration of illness. Echinacea also helps to promote healing, has antiseptic and anti-inflammatory properties, and stimulates the nervous system. It is a very versatile herb and, when taken correctly, can enhance overall health and well-being.

DATA FILE

- **Antiseptic action**
- **Activates white blood cells**
- **Antiviral properties**
- **Enhances resistance to infection**
- **Boosts the immune system**

• Echinacea is a versatile herb, which can be taken internally and applied externally to fight bacterial and viral infections, and can also be used internally to lower fever and calm allergic reactions. Echinacea is one of the most popular immune stimulants, and studies show that it is extremely effective in promoting healing, and fighting such infectious conditions as flu, candidiasis, colds, herpes, and respiratory infections.

• Echinacea also encourages the thymus, bone marrow, and spleen to develop more of their immune cells.

• Echinacea can be taken freeze-dried, as a tincture, or as an extract. Take 25 drops of the tincture, three times daily, or 750mg of the dried root, or 300mg of the dry extract.

• Echinacea is best taken in small, frequent doses. If used in the long term, take for only six days out of seven, or three weeks out of every month, to obtain the best effect.

BELOW *Echinacea is a good supplement for infectious illnesses such as colds and flu.*

ECHINACEA HAS ANTIVIRAL PROPERTIES

TAKE ECHINACEA IF YOU HAVE A TEMPERATURE

BOOST YOUR IMMUNE SYSTEM WITH ECHINACEA

BELOW *Echinacea may be taken freeze-dried or in tincture form. Take in small, frequent doses.*

ECHINACEA TINCTURE

Garlic

Garlic belongs to the onion family, and is one of the oldest cultivated plants in the world. Long used as a medicinal herb, it is one of the best supplements to boost immunity and encourage optimum health. Fresh garlic may be added to the diet, or garlic oil may be taken in capsule form, and it is particularly useful for preventing coronary disease.

BELOW *Supplement your diet with garlic. Eat raw, or lightly cooked, for maximum benefit.*

DATA FILE

- **Cleanses the blood and helps to create and maintain healthy bacteria (flora) in the gut**
- **Helps to bring down fever**
- **Antiseptic, with antibiotic and antifungal actions**
- **Tones the heart and circulatory system**
- **Boosts the immune system**
- **May help to reduce high blood pressure**
- **May prevent some cancers; in particular, stomach cancer**
- **Treats infections of the stomach and respiratory system**
- **Prevents heart disease and reduces the risk of atherosclerosis**
- **Antioxidant**
- **Decongestant**

- Garlic is one of the best-known and most-used medicinal herbs. It is also one of the oldest cultivated plants.
- Its popularity in Mediterranean countries (where heart disease is less common) has encouraged researchers to investigate its role in preventing heart disease, by lowering the level of blood fats.
- Garlic has a strong odor, which many people find off-putting, but its health-giving and preventive properties make it well worth suffering the anti-social effects.
- Effective herbal preparations of garlic can be used at less cost and with fewer side effects than most pharmaceutical drugs, and its use has recently been applauded by the conventional medical establishment.
- Garlic is widely used in cooking, but heat destroys its medicinal effects, so it is more beneficial to use it only slightly cooked, or raw, or to take it in supplement form.
- Suggested daily dosages are 600 to 1,000mg garlic extract or concentrate, or 1,800 to 3,000mg of fresh garlic equivalent.

ABOVE *Garlic is a popular ingredient of the Mediterranean diet; it is grown throughout southern Europe.*

Ginkgo biloba

Ginkgo biloba, described as the world's oldest tree, has been used in Traditional Chinese Medicine for thousands of years, although it is newer to Western therapy. Gingko biloba contains an antioxidant, and is believed to help improve the memory and enhance attentiveness, among other things. It is available as a supplement on its own, or it may be combined with ginseng, or other herbs.

DATA FILE

- **Improves capillary strength and circulation**
- **Has beneficial effects on the blood circulation in the brain**
- **Powerful antioxidant**
- **Reduces damage caused by exposure to radiation**

- Ginkgo biloba is one of the most widely researched medicinal herbs. The Chinese have used the fruits and leaves for thousands of years to treat a variety of health conditions, including asthma, allergies, and coughs. In the West, various compounds have been extracted from ginkgo and synthesized to produce treatments for asthma and other ailments. It has also been used to improve brain function, boost memory, and stimulate alertness. Ginkgo also stimulates the circulation in the brain and ears, and may help to prevent dizziness, hearing loss, tinnitus, stroke, and also depression.
- It is also a powerful antioxidant, and studies show that it may help in the treatment of impotence.
- Ginkgo's effects are due to its high bioflavonoid content, including quercetin, kempferol, and proanthocyanidins.
- Recommended dosage is 40mg, three times daily.

ABOVE *The Chinese people have used ginkgo biloba for thousands of years to treat a wide range of complaints.*

BELOW *Ginkgo biloba, a native plant of the Far East, has become a popular herbal remedy in the West.*

Ginseng

The use of ginseng, like gingko, has come to us from the East. Ginseng root, also known as "man root," because of its shape, is taken to alleviate conditions ranging from old age to sexual debility, and even to improve mental ability. It is "adaptogenic," that is, it acts according to the body's requirements.

BELOW *Ginseng may be taken in capsule form or the dried root may be ground to form a powder.*

CAPSULES

POWDER

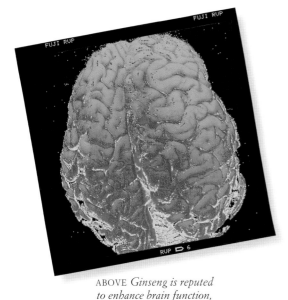

ABOVE *Ginseng is reputed to enhance brain function, improving memory and learning ability.*

DATA FILE

- Stimulates the nervous system and boosts energy
- Stimulates hormone secretion
- Lowers blood-cholesterol levels
- Protects cells from damage due to radiation and exposure to toxins
- Enhances memory, concentration, and learning
- Normalizes physical functioning, and helps to lessen the effects of stress
- Improves liver detoxification function
- Improves appetite, mood, and sleep

- Ginseng is a perennial herb of the genus "Panax." Asiatic ginseng, *P. pseudoginseng*, is native to eastern Asia. Wild American ginseng, *P. quinquefolius*, is native to eastern woodlands of the United States. Dwarf ginseng, *P. trifolus*, is a smaller American species.
- The root of the ginseng plant has for centuries been reputed to be a panacea, particularly for cancer, rheumatism, diabetes, sexual debility, and aging. Today China and Korea export ginseng to the West, where its popularity has grown in recent years. Russian scientists claim to have found substances in ginseng that stimulate endocrine secretions and act as a tonic to the cardiovascular system.

- Ginseng is a source of vitamins, amino acids, and trace elements, and acts on both the cardiovascular and central nervous systems, helping to regulate blood pressure, maintain blood-sugar levels, boost immunity by acting on the thymus and spleen, and encourage blood flow to the brain.
- Ginseng is "adaptogenic," which means that it works according to your body's needs, to create balance.
- In Chinese medicine, ginseng is used to increase deficient "chi," or the vital energy of the body.
- Siberian ginseng is also used as a tonic to enhance balance, and it has additional functions in the body, including making you less susceptible to motion sickness, normalizing high or low blood pressure, stimulating the white cells of the immune system, and a variety of other benefits.
- Ginseng should be taken as directed on the package, and taken three out of four weeks for the best effect.

GINSENG ROOT

Essential Fatty Acids

Essential fatty acids, also called E.F.A.s, are fats required by the body, but not manufactured by it. E.F.A.s work to strengthen the membranes of the cells and to promote the growth of muscles and nerves. Fish oils and evening primrose oil are among the richest dietary sources of essential fatty acids.

ABOVE *Sunflower seeds are rich in omega-6 oils, one of the leading essential fatty acids.*

Natural anti-inflammatories, E.F.A.s are useful in the treatment of arthritis, asthma, and a number of skin conditions. They are also used therapeutically to thin the blood and to prevent blood clotting.

The two main essential fatty acids are linol**eic** acid and linol**enic** acid, also known as omega-6 and omega-3 oils, respectively. Both are vital for the structure and effective working of the brain and nervous system, the immune system, the hormonal system, the cardiovascular system, and the skin. The first sign of their deficiency is a dry skin, dry eyes, and a greater than normal thirst. Seeds in general, but especially sesame and sunflower seeds, are rich in linoleic acid (omega-6), while pumpkin and flax seeds (edible linseeds) are rich in linolenic acid (omega-3).

Linoleic acid (omega-6) is converted in the body into two further substances: gamma-linolenic acid (G.L.A.), and di-homo-gamma-linolenic acid (D.G.L.A.), which is further converted to arachidonic acid (A.A.). Linolenic acid (omega-3) is converted to eicosapentenoic acid (E.P.A.) and docosahexenoic acid (D.H.A.). E.P.A. and D.H.A. are also found in fatty fish (such as mackerel, herring, salmon, sardines). Further to this, D.G.L.A., A.A., and E.P.A. go on to produce prostaglandins *(see p.81).*

FISH OILS

- **Can counteract the effects of some immunosuppressive drugs**
- **May help the treatment of kidney disease**
- **May help to prevent cancer, in particular breast cancer**
- **Stops the progression of arthritis**
- **May help to protect against hypertension**
- **Helps to prevent cardiovascular disease**
- **May help to prevent and treat psoriasis**

- Fish oils contain two long-chain fatty acids called eicosopentenoic acid and docosahexenoic acid that affect the synthesis of prostaglandins, which have a regulatory effect on the body.
- Fish oils are now believed to improve overall health and treat many health conditions.
- The best sources are fish such as herring, salmon, tuna, cod, and prawns.
- For most people it is enough to increase intake of fish and seafood in order to achieve the benefits of the fish oils in the natural form, without taking supplements.

People suffering from arthritis or psoriasis can take up to 4g daily in fish-oil supplements with the supervision of a physician. Maximum suggested dosage for supplements without the supervision of your physician is 900mg per day.

CAUTION

Fish oils may be harmful in diabetics since they can cause an increase in blood sugar and a decline in insulin secretion.

RIGHT *Eat fish, such as salmon, if you wish to increase your intake of essential fatty acids.*

EVENING PRIMROSE OIL

• Reduces scaling and redness, prevents itching, and encourages healing in cases of eczema; also used to treat psoriasis

• Discourages dry skin, and insures that the cellular membranes that make up the skin are stable and strong; there is some evidence that the oil retards the aging process

• May help to prevent multiple sclerosis, and appears to be particularly useful for children suffering from M.S.

• May help treat liver damage caused by alcohol (cirrhosis of the liver), hyperactivity in children, and cystic fibrosis

• May have a stimulating effect on the body, encouraging it to convert fat into energy, which would make it an excellent treatment for obese people

• May ease symptoms of hormonal imbalance, which is perhaps causing conditions such as P.M.S. and menopause problems, by reducing symptoms of bloating, water retention, irritability, and depression

• Reduces inflammation in rheumatoid arthritis

• May have an immuno-suppressive effect on the body

CAUTION

Do not use if you suffer from temporal-lobe epilepsy or manic depression.

EVENING PRIMROSE OIL SUPPLEMENT

• The Native American people were the first to recognize the potential of evening primrose oil as a healer, and they decocted the seeds to make a liquid for healing wounds.

• Evening primrose oil is a rich source of gamma linolenic acid, better known as G.L.A. The body is able to make G.L.A. from essential fatty acids (E.F.A.s), by converting linoleic acid. Evening primrose oil works by providing a natural linoleic acid, which is converted in the body into G.L.A., and by supplying the body with ready-made G.L.A., so it does not have to produce it in such quantities.

• E.F.A.s have numerous functions in the body – one of which is to manufacture hormone-like substances called "prostaglandins," which have important effects on the body, such as toning blood vessels, controlling the action of the digestive system, and brain functioning.

• Prostaglandins also have a beneficial effect on the immune system.

• Evening primrose oil is most often taken in the form of capsules, but it is also available as an oil, and it can be applied to the skin to treat skin conditions. Take 500mg each day for two months, and then for the 10 days preceding each period if you suffer from P.M.S. In menopause, 2,000 to 4,000mg should be taken daily for four weeks, and then 500 to 1,000mg daily thereafter. For asthma, take two 500mg tablets, three times daily, for three to four months, and then one tablet three times daily. If you are taking steroids, this treatment will not work because steroids interfere with evening primrose oil's action.

LEFT *Native Americans boil the seeds of the evening primrose to make a healing liquid.*

ABOVE *The seeds of the evening primrose flower contain gamma-linoleic acid.*

Fiber

Fiber is the indigestible part of plant foods: the "skeleton" that holds the plant together. It offers no nutritional value, but is nonetheless vital in the diet. It helps fill the stomach and move the bowel contents along, at the same time encouraging absorption of nutrients. Too much, however, can loosen the bowel movements, hastening them and inhibiting nutrient takeup.

DATA FILE

- **Reduces the production of cholesterol**
- **May protect against some forms of coronary heart disease**
- **Helps to control diabetes**
- **Helps to control weight**
- **Can be used to treat intestinal disorders such as diverticulitis**
- **Protects against cancers of the colon**

• Dietary fiber is an essential element in the diet even though it provides no nutrients. It consists of plant cellulose and other indigestible materials in foods, along with pectin and gum. The chewing it requires stimulates saliva flow, and the bulk it adds in the stomach and intestines slows down digestion and allows more time for the absorption of nutrients. Diets with sufficient fiber content produce softer, bulkier stools.

• Fiber helps to promote bowel regularity and avoid constipation and other disorders, such as diverticulitis. Studies show that a high-fiber diet can lower the risk of cancers of the colon and rectum, and possibly the breast and prostate as well, since fiber is believed to promote the transit of potentially cancerous substances through the intestine and out of the body. Increased fiber intake may also reduce certain types of free radicals.

• Best sources of dietary fiber include fruits, vegetables, wholegrain breads, and products made from nuts and legumes. An intake of 20 to 60g per day is ideal, and can be taken in the form of food, or as "soluble fiber" at 4 to 6g, which is less likely to cause loose bowel movements. Always take with plenty of water.

LEFT *Help to protect your colon from cancer by including fiber-rich foods, such as apricots, in your diet.*

BELOW *Bread made from wholegrains has much more dietary fiber content than white bread.*

CAUTION

A diet overly abundant in dietary fiber can cut down on the absorption of important trace minerals during digestion by speeding up the transit of food too much. Take a good multivitamin and mineral tablet if you increase your fiber intake significantly.

Polyphenols and Flavonoids

Polyphenols and flavonoids are antioxidants. Red wine offers polyphenols (as does red grape juice and green tea), while flavonoids are found alongside vitamin C in fresh foods such as citrus fruits. These antioxidants strengthen capillary walls, and may help in cases of heavy menstrual bleeding or hemorrhage. Like other antioxidants, they are good detoxifiers.

LEFT *Red wine contains polyphenols, which protect against hemorrhaging and may help cure colds.*

BELOW *Citrus fruits are a good source of flavonoids, particularly the central white core of the fruit.*

DATA FILE

- **Reduce bruising in susceptible individuals**
- **Protect capillaries**
- **Protect against cerebral and other hemorrhaging**
- **Reduce menstrual bleeding**
- **Have antioxidant properties** (*see pp. 18–19*) **and encourage vitamin C's own antioxidant qualities**
- **Antiviral activity**
- **Anti-inflammatory**
- **Antiallergy**
- **May help to cure colds**

• Polyphenols, also known as polyphenolic flavonoids, are powerful antioxidants related to tannins. Green tea, and red grapes in the form of red wine and grape juice, are rich in polyphenols, and supplements containing extracts of these substances can now be bought.

• Flavonoids, also known as bioflavonoids and flavones, were originally called vitamin P. They are antioxidants, found in the company of vitamin C in natural foods, and are responsible for the color in the leaves, flowers, and stems of food plants.

There are 12 basic classes of flavonoids, and in addition to their antioxidant qualities, they are known to help strengthen capillary walls, and may be useful in the treatment of heavy menstrual bleeding. Some flavonoids, such as quercetin, rutin, green tea, and curcumin, have anti-inflammatory properties, which help to form prosta-glandins (*see p. 81*).

• Best sources include citrus fruits (the central white core is the richest in bioflavonoids), apricots, cherries, green bell peppers, broccoli, lemons.

• Flavonoids are not toxic, and should be taken with vitamin C for best effect. Supplements come in the form of quercetin, usually derived from algae, and rutin, in supplements of 250 to 500mg. More popular products are the bioflavonoid complex, and individual bioflavonoids in combination with other supplements, commonly vitamin C, which has a protective effect. These are usually found in dosages that range from 500 to 1,000mg.

• Some herbs are also rich in polyphenols and flavonoids, including ginkgo biloba (*see p. 82*), hawthorn, milk thistle, and bilberry.

Supplements for Overall Good Health

EXCITING DEVELOPMENTS in the study of nutrition have meant that more and more of us are taking nutritional supplements. Even healthy diets may no longer have the requisite nutritional elements, and in order to have immune systems that are strong enough to fight off disease, and to have optimum levels of energy and mental acuity, we must find these elements elsewhere.

For thousands of years, people have been aware of the connections between foods, diet, and health, but it wasn't until the 20th century that the vital elements of food were isolated and identified. Nutritional medicine, that is the use of nutrition to prevent illness and attain good health, is, therefore, a relatively new science, and we are only now beginning to understand how our eating habits, and the food we eat, have an impact on our health. Studies now show that nutritional substances can not only maintain health, by preventing deficiency diseases, but also act to insure optimum functioning of all the organs and systems in our body.

They are now known to boost immunity, stimulate our mental performance, extend our lives, and prevent serious health diseases, such as heart disease, immune conditions, and cancer.

ABOVE *The whole family can benefit from nutritional therapy, from the elderly to the very young.*

LEFT *There are special treatment programs designed for babies and young children.*

ALWAYS GET ADVICE

In the hands of a trained practitioner, nutritional treatment is one of the safest complementary therapies available. You should always be wary of extreme diets, or those that are restrictive in any way, concentrating on eating moderate amounts of fresh, unprocessed nutritious foods that are as free as possible from chemicals. Nutritional therapy should always be undertaken on the advice of a registered practitioner and he or she should be aware of every other

aspect of your physical and mental condition. There are many ailments that contraindicate the use of certain supplements (that is, they would be dangerous) and it is essential that your therapist is aware of everything that may affect your health. People of any age can benefit from the prudent use of nutritional therapy, and there are special treatment programs designed for babies, pregnant women, children, the elderly, and those with chronic, serious health conditions.

IS YOUR SUPPLEMENTATION PROGRAM WORKING?

Your body will soon tell you whether your supplements are working. Do your symptoms return when you stop taking your supplements, and do they go away again when you restart? Do you feel nauseous or suffer from stomach pain after taking your supplements? You need to understand why you are taking each supplement in order to recognize whether or not it is doing its job. If you have a chronic health condition, or have multiple symptoms or health problems, see a nutritionist for advice.

SUPPLEMENT SAFETY

If you exercise caution, and follow the recommended doses for vitamins, minerals, and other supplements, they will be almost completely danger-free. No commonly used drugs can equal the safety and effectiveness of nutritional compounds. Vitamins can be beneficial in the treatment of virtually all chronic diseases, even those for which no effective drugs are yet known. In fact, vitamins in sufficient doses, taken under the supervision of trained nutritionists or dieticians, can help you to cut down or eliminate some of the drugs you may be taking. Do not, however, expect your own physician to know how to use nutrients to treat disease, and do not even consider giving up necessary medication in favor of supplements, without the supervision of your physician and a trained, registered therapist.

Overdoses that require medical attention will produce symptoms well in advance of any serious toxic reaction. Warning signs include dry skin, severe headaches, hair loss,

ABOVE *Supplements can treat chronic diseases. They may even help to reduce your medication.*

stiff joints, or tingling (pins and needles) in your extremities. If you suddenly suffer from any one of these conditions, discontinue use immediately, and see your practitioner for advice.

Don't try to take every piece of advice given here for your condition: pick and choose among the suggestions for the therapy you believe will suit you and your particular lifestyle.

BELOW *Even healthy diets may need supplementing with vitamins and minerals to insure optimum health.*

ZUCCHINI

CURLY KALE

APPLE

NEW POTATOES

BANANA

CARROT

SUPPLEMENT

GRAPES

ORANGE

PEAR

PARSNIP

Boost your Immune System

A STRONG IMMUNE SYSTEM *prevents illness and allergies, helps you to fight off infections and infestations, and insures that you recover from illness quickly and efficiently. There are a number of nutritional elements that will help to keep it strong, and functioning well.*

The immune system forms the body's defense against foreign substances, such as micro-organisms (bacteria, fungi, viruses, and parasites, for example), potentially toxic molecules, or abnormal cells (virus-infected or malignant). Under normal circumstances the immune system responds to foreign organisms by producing antibodies, which kill off invading organisms and neutralize their toxic products (toxins). A major function of the immune system in maintaining good health is surveillance of the cells of the body to insure that they are not abnormal.

WEAKENING FACTORS

Your immune system can become impaired by the following factors:
- injuries
- surgery
- the overuse of antibiotics, which can suppress the immune system and destroy the flora, the healthy bacteria of the bowel
- some drugs
- digestive disorders, such as Candida, enzyme deficiencies, and chronic constipation
- poor diet
- pollution
- stress
- genetic problems
- disease
- inherited weaknesses

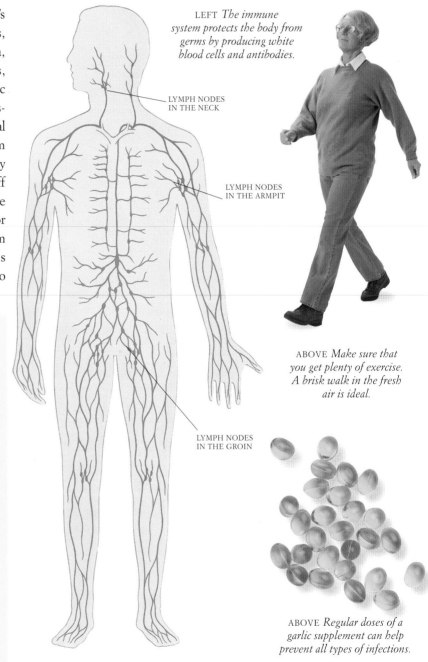

LEFT *The immune system protects the body from germs by producing white blood cells and antibodies.*

LYMPH NODES
IN THE NECK

LYMPH NODES
IN THE ARMPIT

LYMPH NODES
IN THE GROIN

ABOVE *Make sure that you get plenty of exercise. A brisk walk in the fresh air is ideal.*

ABOVE *Regular doses of a garlic supplement can help prevent all types of infections.*

IMMUNE-BOOSTING NUTRIENTS AND SUPPLEMENTS

• Garlic helps to prevent infections of all kinds, including those that have become immune to antibiotics. It also helps to cleanse the blood. Take 1,000 to 1,500mg of pure or concentrated garlic or garlic powder per day to boost immunity.

• Echinacea is widely used to treat chronic and acute infections, and to boost the immune system. It cleanses the blood and lymphatic system, which stimulates the production of white blood cells and antibodies. The easiest way to take echinacea is at 25 drops of tincture, three times daily, with food. Take three weeks on, and one week off.

• Ginseng can boost immunity and encourage the body to deal efficiently with stress, as well as stimulating white-blood-cell production, and aiding recovery after illness. Take 250 to 500mg, once or twice daily.

• Vitamin A and beta-carotene boost immunity by increasing both the number and the activity of antibodies such as T-helper cells. They also help the thymus gland to grow, protecting it from the harmful effects of stress. Vitamin A protects the respiratory system from viral infections, and beta-carotene is an antioxidant, with a good immune-enhancing effect. Try to take 5,000 to 10,000iu vitamin A, plus 25,000 to 50,000iu beta-carotene, daily.

• Vitamin B6 can help to keep your immune system functioning well, and may help to prevent cancer and the growth of other tumors. Take 25 to 50mg daily, as part of a B-complex tablet.

• Vitamin C helps the body resist infection, and it works to aid the thymus gland and white blood cells. Take 250 to 500mg, two or three times daily, to boost immunity.

• Vitamin E is an immune stimulant that can encourage the body to resist a number of diseases, including some cancers and autoimmune conditions. It also improves antibody response. To boost your immune system, take 400 to 600iu daily.

• Zinc is necessary for the immune system to function properly, and it can prevent a number of viruses from spreading. To boost your immune system, take 25mg daily.

• Selenium boosts the immune system, largely through antioxidant activity, and can protect the integrity of the cells, improving their overall function. To boost your immune system, take 50 to 200mcg daily, in combination with vitamin E.

• Royal jelly boosts immunity, as does propolis and bee pollen. Propolis in particular may help to prevent infection in the throat. Take the recommended dosage daily, unless you are allergic to bee products.

• Astragalus can be used to increase energy levels and resistance to disease. Take 250 to 500mg two or three times daily.

GINSENG

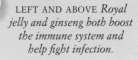

ROYAL JELLY

LEFT AND ABOVE *Royal jelly and ginseng both boost the immune system and help fight infection.*

ABOVE *Make sure that you drink lots of fresh bottled water, at least six glasses every day.*

WHAT YOU CAN DO TO HELP

◆ Make sure that you have plenty of sleep.
◆ Drink lots of fresh, bottled water, which helps to cleanse the system.
◆ Get plenty of exercise.
◆ Eat a balanced diet, rich in wholefoods, nuts and seeds, fresh vegetables and fruits, and which is high in fiber and low in saturated fat, and avoid smoking, refined grains, sweeteners, alcohol, environmental pollutants, which all compromise immune activity.
◆ Take a good multivitamin and mineral supplement to insure that you have adequate quantities of nutrients with immune-boosting activity. These include vitamins A, B-complex, C, E, and the minerals zinc and selenium (*see opposite*).

Increase your Energy Levels

STUDIES SHOW THAT *the majority of cases of "chronic" fatigue are caused by nutritional deficiencies. Physicians report that the number of patients who complain of being tired all the time (now known as T.A.T., or Tired All the Time syndrome) is increasing, and scientific evidence indicates that this constant fatigue is almost entirely related to deficiencies (even subclinical deficiencies) of various nutrients.*

The increased use of stimulants, such as caffeine, nicotine, and even amphetamines, puts an enormous strain on the body. Although most of us use such substances as instant "pick-me-ups" they do, in the end, exacerbate fatigue, often producing the very symptoms we are trying to alleviate, such as drowsiness, a shorter attention span, and an overall lack of energy. There are a number of natural substances which will work to boost our energy levels by improving overall body function, and others which work through the nervous and circulatory systems in particular to increase alertness, and provide the stimulus necessary for a sustained and deliberate release of energy.

If you suffer from recurrent fatigue, however, it is important to analyze your diet and lifestyle before considering supplements. If your lifestyle exposes you to a large number of toxins, perhaps in the form of pollution, smoking, a diet of low quality foods, or excessive intake of alcohol, it is essential that you take steps to remove these substances as they may be a contributory factor if not the cause, of the problem. Try to drink plenty of fresh, filtered water, which will help flush toxins from your body and replenish body tissue that has become dehydrated through overuse of stimulants.

ABOVE *Ginger has stimulating properties and may help to boost your natural energy levels.*

ABOVE *Take a daily tincture of gingko biloba to improve brain function and boost memory.*

LEFT *Avoid caffeine and foods that are high in fat. Any stimulating effects that they might have will be shortlived.*

SUPPLEMENTS TO BOOST ENERGY LEVELS

• Ginseng strengthens and normalizes the body, and studies show that it both encourages energy levels and improves mental performance. Regular use is advised, because its effects build up over time. Take 500 to 1,000mg daily.

• Gingko biloba is said to improve brain function and to boost memory and alertness. Take daily in tincture form, or in tablets – about 40g three times daily.

• Ginger has a stimulating effect on the body – particularly the circulation and digestive system – and may help to boost energy levels. Take 25 drops of tincture, three times daily, or 500 to 1,000mg of the dried herb. (Fresh ginger is not concentrated enough).

• Oats are a nutritious, healing herb with an affinity to the nervous system – working both to stimulate and restore. You can take oats daily in a tincture form, or try to eat plenty of organic oats in your diet.

• Gotu kola is a traditional restorative for the nervous system and will help to increase energy and endurance. Take 12 drops of the tincture, three times daily.

• Iron is necessary for the production of energy, and for immune function, and forms part of the hemoglobin that carries oxygen in the bloodstream. It is often used therapeutically for fatigue. Take 10 to 15mg daily.

• B-complex vitamins are essential for the functioning of the nervous system, and help to boost energy levels. Take 50 to 100mg daily, as a B-complex formula.

• Magnesium works to create energy by breaking down sugar stores in the liver, and it is also necessary for strong, healthy bones. Supplements are often used to treat fatigue, and should be taken with calcium, at about 450 to 650mg per day.

• Coenzyme Q10 is essential for the production of energy and helps the cells to use energy efficiently. It is also a mild metabolic stimulant, and should be taken in doses from 30 to 50mg daily.

• Royal jelly is an enormously nutritious product, and it is often taken as a supplement to boost energy levels, largely because it is said to deal with any underlying deficiencies that may be causing energy to flag. It also acts to support the adrenal gland, which is seriously depleted by stress. Take 200 to 500mg daily to boost energy levels.

ABOVE *Include organic oats in your diet to restore the nervous system.*

ABOVE *Total relaxation is extremely important. Try yoga or meditation.*

WHAT YOU CAN DO TO HELP

♦ Try to get plenty of regular sleep, and avoid drinking alcohol before retiring, as it can discourage restful sleep.

♦ Avoid caffeine and any other artificial stimulants, which offer momentary boosts, but which leave you more tired once their effects have worn off.

♦ Take a good multivitamin and mineral supplement, to insure that you are getting enough of the required nutrients.

♦ Eat a diet that is rich in fresh, wholefoods, and low in fats (which can make you sleepy).

♦ Get some exercise every day, which helps to increase circulation and encourage all body systems to work more efficiently.

♦ Make enough time to relax properly, perhaps through meditation or yoga.

Prevent and Treat Cancer

THE FREE RADICALS THAT *cause aging (see pp. 18–19) are also the cause of many cancers. By eating a diet that is rich in antioxidants, which effectively "mop up" free radicals, we can do a great deal to prevent the disease, and to halt its course. This revelation is one of the most important landmarks in the study of cancer.*

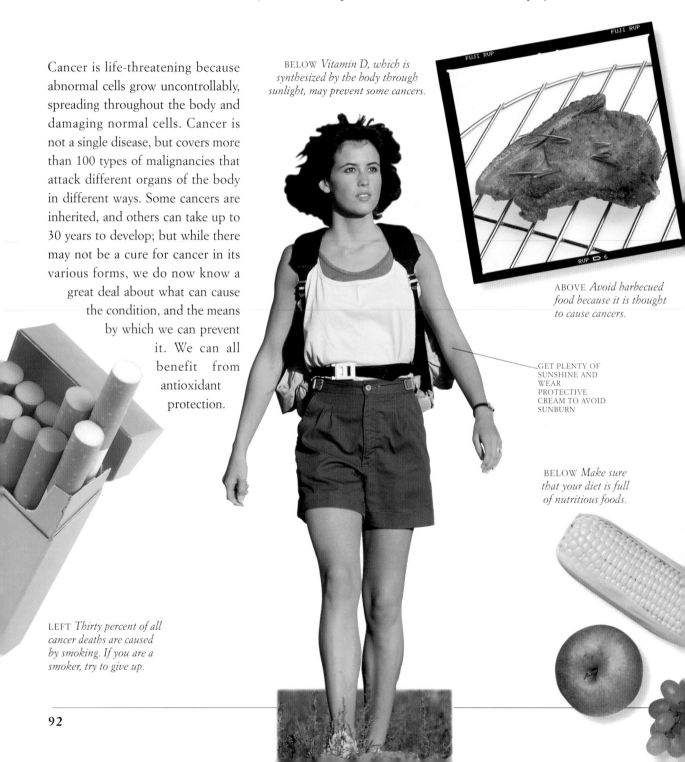

Cancer is life-threatening because abnormal cells grow uncontrollably, spreading throughout the body and damaging normal cells. Cancer is not a single disease, but covers more than 100 types of malignancies that attack different organs of the body in different ways. Some cancers are inherited, and others can take up to 30 years to develop; but while there may not be a cure for cancer in its various forms, we do now know a great deal about what can cause the condition, and the means by which we can prevent it. We can all benefit from antioxidant protection.

BELOW *Vitamin D, which is synthesized by the body through sunlight, may prevent some cancers.*

ABOVE *Avoid barbecued food because it is thought to cause cancers.*

GET PLENTY OF SUNSHINE AND WEAR PROTECTIVE CREAM TO AVOID SUNBURN

BELOW *Make sure that your diet is full of nutritious foods.*

LEFT *Thirty percent of all cancer deaths are caused by smoking. If you are a smoker, try to give up.*

SUPPLEMENTS TO PREVENT AND TREAT CANCER

• Insure that you get some sunlight each day, and plenty of vitamin D in the diet. Vitamin D is linked with reduced risk of a number of cancers. Take up to 400iu per day to decrease your risk of getting cancer.

• Calcium can help to protect the colon and the rectum from cancer. Take between 800 and 1,500mg daily.

• Zinc can help to protect the body from cancer, and should be taken at 17 to 25mg daily.

• B-complex vitamins protect against the risk of a number of cancers, and are crucial to immune functioning. Take 25 to 50mg once or twice daily.

• Antioxidant vitamins A, C, and E have been proved to have significant cancer-preventive effects. Take a good supplement daily.

• The antioxidant mineral selenium helps boost immunity. Take 100 to 200mcg per day.

• Vitamin C reduces the risk of cancers, and has been shown to offer protection against many others. Take 250 to 500mg, two to three times daily.

• Vitamin A and beta-carotene are linked with reduced cancer rates. Beta-carotene in particular is useful, for it offers the most protection by boosting the immune system and neutralizing free radicals. Take 5 to 10,000iu of vitamin A, plus 25,000 to 45,000iu of beta-carotene daily.

• Vitamin E can enhance the effectiveness of chemotherapy and radiotherapy, and it may impede the growth of some types of cancers. As an antioxidant, it also reduces the risk of many cancers. Take 400 to 600iu daily.

• Garlic has strong anticancer effects and contains a number of substances that neutralize carcinogens. Take 600 to 1,000mg pure or concentrated garlic or garlic extract powder daily.

• Coenzyme Q10 has been shown to reduce the adverse effects of chemotherapy. Take 30mg daily.

• E.F.A.s (essential fatty acids) reduce the risk of breast and other cancers. Take a daily dose of 500 to 1,000mg.

• *Acidophilus* and other beneficial bacteria products can reduce the risk of colon cancer. Take the dosage recommended on the package at least once a day, before eating.

• Fiber supplements can help to prevent cancer particularly in the gastrointestinal tract, and can help to reduce toxins formed in the intestines that may be cancer precursors. Fiber supplements should be taken at 4 to 6g every day.

WHAT YOU CAN DO TO HELP

• Stop smoking. People who smoke are more than 10 times more likely to develop lung cancer, and up to 30 percent of all cancer deaths are caused by smoking.

• Cut down on alcohol. Heavy alcohol consumption increases your risk of cancers of the liver, mouth, esophagus, and larynx. Try to drink no more than two units of alcohol each day.

• Eat plenty of fiber, which can help prevent many cancers.

• Eat at least five servings of fruits and vegetables each day since they contain important antioxidant vitamins and minerals.

• Take a good vitamin and mineral supplement that contains vitamins C, E, and other antioxidant vitamins and minerals that can help to neutralize certain carcinogens. Supplements can also boost your immune system, so that it can destroy newly formed cancer cells before they multiply.

• Cut down on fat in your diet. A high-fat diet is related to the promotion of several types of tumors.

• Avoid deep-fried and barbecued foods, both of which can cause cancer. Also avoid large amounts of smoked, salt-pickled, and salt-cured foods

because they can increase your risk of cancer of the stomach.

• Avoid sunburning. Skin cancer is caused primarily by sunburn.

• Eat a good diet. Up to 40 percent of cancer patients actually die of malnutrition because cancer cells release a hormone that suppresses the appetite. Nausea and vomiting caused by treatment can also exacerbate the problem. Even if you are not hungry, try to eat at least a little nutritious food each day.

• Find a support group to share your worries. Stress can lower immune activity and energy levels, among other things, which can make your body less likely to deal adequately with carcinogens and cancer cells.

Live Longer

SCIENTISTS ARE NOW *able to pinpoint the physical indications of aging, and the various stages at which they occur, and to some extent are able to ascertain why they occur. While experts still do not understand why we age, and why degeneration in the body occurs, they do know what causes some of the problems normally associated with aging, and they are able to retard or halt the degenerative processes associated with aging.*

We age in a variety of ways, some of which are very visible, including a decline in height, shrinkage of muscle, thinning and graying of hair, and wrinkling of our skin. Internally, there is the progressive loss of cells in the brain, kidneys, and other vital organs. Important tissues – ranging from the muscles to the brain – shrink and become less competent with age. Many of these changes are reflected in the decline of body functions, including hearing, eyesight, immunity to infection, and circulation, the last of which is needed for oxygenated blood to get around our bodies.

There is no doubt that we will all age – for there is nothing to stop the passage of time – but there are ways to hold back the ravages of time, and the degenerative effects of aging. Scientists confirm that the human body should have a lifespan of 110 years, although very few of us last that long. Here's what you can do to get there.

RIGHT *Eat plenty of fruits and vegetables that are rich in vitamin C and have antioxidant effects.*

LEFT *Include mono-unsaturated oils, such as olive oil, in your diet. They help protect against heart disease.*

SUPPLEMENTS TO HELP YOU LIVE LONGER

• Beta-carotene, as an antioxidant, can help to prevent cell damage, and will boost immunity and protect against disease associated with aging. Insure that you get 25,000 to 50,000iu per day.

• Vitamin C is a powerful antioxidant, particularly for the brain. It also reduces the risk of cancer, heart disease, cataracts, and other degenerative diseases. Insure that you get 250 to 500mg of vitamin C two or three times daily.

• Vitamin E works as an antioxidant, and can increase your lifespan. Even low levels of supplementation can help to prevent cancer and heart disease. You should try to get 400 to 600iu per day.

• Selenium is the other most important antioxidant, and it has now been proved that it decreases the rate of cancer, and increases lifespan. Take in combination with vitamin E, at 100 to 200mcg per day.

• Ginseng energizes and strengthens, and is, in the East, called the root of immortality. It is both rejuvenating and a tonic, and boosts immune activity, brain function, and reduces symptoms of fatigue. You'll need 250 to 500mg per day for best effect.

• Gingko biloba is used by the Chinese to promote longevity. It is known to alleviate the symptoms associated with aging, such as poor memory and hearing. Use as directed on the package, three times daily.

• Garlic reduces the risk of heart disease, and acts as an antioxidant. Try to supplement 1,000mg of pure or concentrated garlic per day.

WHAT YOU CAN DO TO HELP

◆ If you use a daily sunscreen, your body will repair some of the damage caused by earlier exposure, and you'll look younger. Sunscreen prevents age spots and wrinkles, and skin cancer.

◆ Work on boosting your immune system *(see pp. 88–89).*

◆ There is no question that the best thing you can do for your body is to exercise. Research shows that exercise can reverse the results of aging. Exercise for about 20 minutes, three times a week, ensuring that you are giving your heart and lungs a good workout, and you can lose up to 20 years. Weight-bearing exercise will prevent diseases such as osteoporosis. Exercise can also prevent age-related conditions such as heart disease, overweight, high blood pressure, and high cholesterol levels.

◆ Most leafy green and brightly colored vegetables contain a substance called beta-carotene, a type of vitamin A that acts as an antioxidant *(see below).* Beta-carotene has been proved to prevent cancer and heart attacks.

◆ Fruits and vegetables rich in vitamin C improve health overall, and the antioxidant benefits can help to retard the aging process. Eat plenty of citrus fruits, red bell peppers, cabbage, tomatoes, spinach, and broccoli.

◆ Eating a high-fiber diet will encourage a clean bowel, which allows the body's natural, healthy bacteria (called flora) to flourish. Flora are required to fight off disease and infections.

◆ Reduce your intake of saturated fats, which clog arteries and cause weight gain. Eat healthy fats, such as olive oil, and make sure that less than 30 percent of your diet takes the form of fat.

◆ Drink plenty of water. Water hydrates your system, insures the speedy elimination of toxins, acts as a mild diuretic, and cleanses the body.

◆ A high-fiber diet also stimulates the digestive tract and reduces the incidence of cancers – particularly of the digestive system.

◆ Watch your caffeine levels – and that means tea, coffee, and chocolate. Caffeine has been linked to high cholesterol and blood pressure, P.M.S. (premenstrual syndrome), insomnia, and some breast disease. It also artificially stimulates your central nervous system, which raises adrenaline levels *(see Stress below).*

◆ One of the greatest causes of aging is stress, which places incredible physical, mental, and psychological demands on our bodies. Stress has now been linked to premature aging, high blood pressure, heart disease, and the niggling ailments that we associate with age, including insomnia, digestive problems, skin complaints, as well as aches and pains. Stress has also been proved to reduce the power of our immune systems. *(See pp. 100–101 for supplements that help you to cope with the effects of stress.)*

◆ Attempt to cut down on stress, which reduces your ability to concentrate and make decisions.

◆ Evidence proves that both the mind and body benefit from a good night's sleep – you will perform at optimum levels and your appearance will improve. The greatest concentration of growth hormones are released at night, which helps our bodies to repair and rejuvenate. Everyone needs a different amount of sleep, and your individual level will be whatever is necessary for you to feel rested and able to function best the next day.

◆ Avoid smoking, which causes wrinkles, reduces lung capacity (and makes it more difficult to get oxygen to those needy cells), and is a primary cause of cancer.

◆ Don't drink too much alcohol, which can affect brain cells and cause irreversible brain damage.

◆ Use your mind! Change the way that you do things occasionally. Try to meet new and stimulating people. Change hobbies or read a different kind of book. All stimulation works to spark brain function.

◆ Be happy! If you are fulfilled and leading an exciting, stimulating life, you are more likely to live longer. The strong relationship between the mind and the body means that when you feel great, you'll look great, and you'll be more likely to achieve optimum health.

RIGHT *Keep your mind active. Stimulate your brain by learning a new skill or taking up a new hobby.*

Achieve your Natural Weight

BEING OVERWEIGHT *Can be uncomfortable and make you unhappy, not to mention, ultimately, ill. We all have a natural weight that suits us – and it is not stick-thin – and the way to begin to achieve it is to think of food as a friend, not an enemy. Food in the right amounts is very, very good for us.*

The secret to losing weight is not, as countless experts over the past decades have insisted, through calorie-counting diets. Calorie counting requires an attitude of self-denial and an artificial, obsessive approach to food. It is rarely an effective way of maintaining lower weight, and if you drastically cut down your calorie intake for more than 10 days, your body thinks it is being starved and reacts by slowing down – and a slower metabolism means that you need less fuel, or food, to maintain your body weight. And it's not fat that your body burns when it thinks it's starving, it's muscle, and that's what we need to burn calories.

Losing weight naturally can be achieved by changing your attitude to food and making an effort to become fit. When you are fit, you are able to burn calories far more efficiently, and you can actually eat more without putting on excess weight. Changing your attitude should involve listening to your body, which means eating when you are hungry, rather than at pre-ordained times, and eating foods that "feel" right, as long as this is a real need rather than one created in the mind.

A recurrent weight problem may be linked to nutritional deficiency, or body systems that are not working at optimum level. There are a variety of supplements that may help.

ABOVE *If you eat complex carbohydrate foods, rather than high-fat ones, you can eat large quantities without putting on weight.*

DON'T EAT WHEN YOU ARE AGITATED OR EXCITED

MAIN MEALS ARE BEST EATEN AT MIDDAY NOT LATE AT NIGHT

BELOW *Rushing your food, and eating late at night in front of the television, are all factors which may prevent weight loss.*

WHAT YOU CAN DO TO HELP

◆ Eat at least five servings of fresh fruit and vegetables each day. Work your other foods around them, concentrating on quality rather than quantity and ensuring that you don't eat more than approximately 30g of fat each day.

◆ Eat little and often, which gives your body a chance to digest and process the energy from your food more efficiently. It is better to eat your largest meal at midday, which gives your body time to digest and use it before sleeping.

◆ Listen to your body and eat when you are hungry.

◆ Base your diet on fresh, unrefined wholefoods.

◆ Don't eat just before going to bed.

◆ Eat for the purpose of being healthy and active, and in order to get energy. Don't eat for the sake of it.

◆ Enjoy your food. Food is sensual, and you don't need a lot to experience its effects. Eat a healthy diet, with small quantities of treats when you want them. You'll find that if you eat well, your cravings for sweet and fatty things will diminish, and are more easily satisfied.

◆ Drink at least six glasses of fresh water each day, which will help the body to flush out toxins and cleanse the digestive system, making it work more effectively.

◆ Join an exercise class, or find a form of exercise that you can fit into a busy lifestyle. Walking is the newest approved form of exercise. Walking for only 30 minutes per day, at a brisk pace, burns off more than 2,000 calories a week, with the added benefit of making you fit.

◆ Work on improving your self-esteem. Hold yourself correctly. Wear clothes that fit. A good attitude may make you feel more energetic, which translates itself into an improved sense of well-being. Studies show that when you are feeling well, you are less hungry and tired – which in turn may help you to lose unwanted pounds.

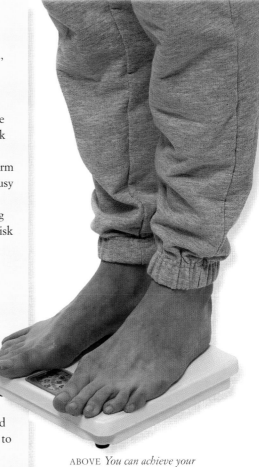

ABOVE *You can achieve your natural weight without calorie counting. Just eat sensibly.*

SUPPLEMENTS TO HELP YOU ACHIEVE YOUR NATURAL WEIGHT

• There is some evidence that bee pollen, which is available as a powder or in tablet form, may stimulate the metabolism and suppress the appetite. Don't use this if you are allergic to bee stings or honey.

• Brewer's yeast may reduce cravings for sweet food.

• The amino acid phenylalanine has been recommended for weight loss. Take 100 to 500mg daily, on an empty stomach at night.

• A mild chromium deficiency may cause cravings and a drop in blood sugar. Take a supplement each day to regulate blood-sugar levels.

• *Acidophilus* and other healthy bacteria can help to enhance digestion, which means that nutrients are better absorbed and waste is better eliminated.

• Coenzyme Q10 helps the body's cells use oxygen and generate energy. There is some evidence that people supplementing CoQ10 are able to lose weight more quickly. Take 15 to 30mg each day.

• Fiber can help to promote weight loss by filling the stomach, and by stimulating the release of hormones that suppress appetite. Fiber also promotes the transportation of fats and calories through the digestive system, lowering the amount absorbed by the blood and stored in the body. Take 4 to 5g daily, and make sure you get plenty of natural sources of fiber in your food.

• Ginger and cinnamon (and other heat-producing herbs and spices) temporarily increase body temperature and help to encourage weight loss.

• B-complex vitamins have been linked with improved function of the thyroid gland, and with fat metabolism. Insure that you get 25 to 50mg, twice daily.

Improve your Memory

MANY FACTORS CAN *affect your memory, including stress, illness, aging, drinking too much, exercising too little, and eating badly. Thankfully, there is plenty you can do to enhance memory function and boost mental agility, both through diet, lifestyle, and, when necessary, supplementation with a wide range of unique herbs and nutrients.*

One of the symptoms of an overloaded system, increased levels of stress, and, indeed, aging, is reduced mental performance. Our brains need a good blood supply in order to function at their best, and a number of illnesses that cause memory and mental-function problems limit the flow of blood to the brain. There are no drugs available that can encourage memory or brain function, but there are many supplements and nutrients, often prescribed by physicians, that can do just that.

When the brain and the nervous system are working at optimum level, we will be able to operate at our peak mental ability. Severe nutritional deficiencies have been known to cause mental problems, and even marginal deficiencies can prevent the brain from functioning at optimum level.

Overuse of alcohol can also affect memory, and damage the cells of the brain and nervous system, but there are, fortunately, ways to limit the damage of alcohol and other toxins on brain function.

LEFT *Alcohol can damage the brain and nervous system. Limit your intake.*

ABOVE *Eat foods that are rich in B-vitamins for the brain. Deficiency can lead to memory loss, mental confusion, and depression.*

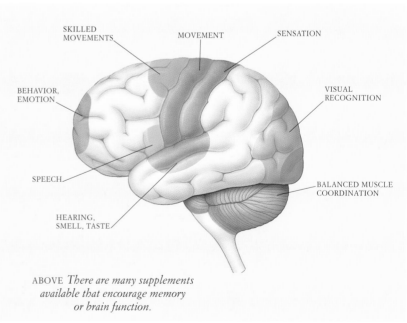

SKILLED MOVEMENTS

MOVEMENT

SENSATION

BEHAVIOR, EMOTION

VISUAL RECOGNITION

SPEECH

BALANCED MUSCLE COORDINATION

HEARING, SMELL, TASTE

ABOVE *There are many supplements available that encourage memory or brain function.*

ABOVE *Try to cut down on your intake of soft drinks. They contain harmful toxins.*

WHAT YOU CAN DO TO HELP

♦ Avoid drinking too much alcohol, which can damage the brain and nervous system. Avoid smoking, which also has a negative effect on brain power in the long term.

♦ Eat plenty of fresh fruits and vegetables, for their antioxidant properties, and cut down on toxins (found in convenience foods, additives and preservatives, soft drinks, and so on).

♦ Make sure you get plenty of sleep. Sleep deprivation can cause memory problems, and decreased mental efficiency.

♦ Get lots of exercise, which can improve circulation to the brain and nervous system, and help you to relax. Studies show that regular exercise boosts short-term memory.

SUPPLEMENTS TO IMPROVE YOUR MEMORY

• The B vitamins are the most important vitamins for the brain and the nervous system, and they promote their operation. Studies have shown that deficiencies of folic acid and the other B vitamins can lead to memory loss, mental confusion, depression, and cognitive impairment. Take 25 to 50mg twice daily.

• Zinc helps to prevent damage to the brain caused by free radicals *(see pp. 52–53)*, and it also improves the function of the neurotransmitters. People with zinc deficiencies have decreased memory and attention spans. Take 17 to 25mg each day.

• Magnesium helps the nervous system to function and helps to transmit nerve signals. Take 450 to 650mg each day, with twice as much calcium, as the optimum level for brain and nervous-system function.

• Vitamin C is required for the production of neurotransmitters and, as an antioxidant, helps to prevent damage to the brain cells by oxidation. Take 250 to 500mg, two or three times daily.

• Choline and lecithin can directly affect the neurotransmitters in the brain and are positively linked with good memory. Choline is available in many forms and should be taken at 100 to 200mg per day. Take 1 to 2 tablespoons of lecithin granules.

• Gingko biloba increases circulation to all parts of the body – including the brain – and has been shown to enhance brain power and memory. It is also an antioxidant, which helps to prevent damage to the cells of the brain. Take daily, as per recommended dosage.

• Ginseng can increase alertness and mental performance and has a stimulating effect. One study shows that ginseng allows people to work longer and harder at mental jobs, with a lower level of mistakes. Take 500 to 1,000mg daily, as required for a short-term boost.

• Gotu kola is used to strengthen the nervous system, and it may also improve memory and help to enhance mental performance. Take as directed on the package.

RIGHT *Plenty of deep, restful sleep is invaluable. Too little sleep can cause impaired mental function.*

Deal with Stress

STRESS IS A MAJOR factor in diseases where physical symptoms are prompted by mental or emotional problems. Indeed, stress-related disorders make up 50 to 80 percent of all illnesses, though stress may not be the only cause. Illnesses affected by stress include high blood pressure, heart disease, arthritis, asthma, insomnia and other sleep disturbances, eating disorders, eczema, and ulcers.

Stress is not actually an illness in itself, but rather a response by the body to anything that puts a strain upon it. Many illnesses can be triggered by or exacerbated by stress.

Most of us think of tense situations and worries as being the major cause of stress. In reality, stresses can be far more profound and wide ranging, and can include environmental stresses, such as pollution, noise, housing problems, cold or overheating; physical stresses, such

ABOVE *Stress can take many forms, including environmental pollution.*

as illnesses, injuries, an inadequate diet or one that is too high in refined foods, additives or toxins such as alcohol or caffeine; and mental stresses, such as problems in a relationship, financial worries, job difficulties or redundancy, and many, many more.

All of these factors have an effect on our body, causing it to make a series of rapid physiological changes, called "adaptive responses," in order to deal with threatening or demanding situations.

ABOVE *Illnesses or injuries can put a strain on our mental and physical well-being.*

RIGHT *Mental problems, such as difficulties in a relationship, cause a great amount of stress.*

LEFT *Stretch the body to relieve tension in the muscles and to teach you to breathe efficiently.*

SUPPLEMENTS TO DEAL WITH STRESS

• Eating a good, balanced diet will make your body stronger and able to cope more efficiently with stress. B-vitamins are often depleted by stress, so insure that you are getting enough in your diet, or take a good supplement.

• There is some evidence that bee and flower pollen, available in tablets or in grains, can boost immunity and energize the body. Don't take them if you think you are allergic to honey or bee stings.

• An amino acid called L-tyrosine appears to energize and relieve stress, and studies show that people taking this supplement react better to stressful situations, staying more alert, less anxious, more efficient, and having fewer complaints about physical discomforts.

• Vitamin C is a great stress reliever, and boosts immunity, making you fitter and more healthy.

• Herbs that encourage relaxation and act as a tonic to the nervous system include balm, lavender, chamomile, verbena, passiflora, and oats. Any of these can be drunk as an infusion – as often as necessary in stressful situations.

• Ginseng is an excellent "adaptogenic" herb, which means that it lifts you when you are tired, and relaxes you when you are stressed. It also works on the immune system and energizes. Some therapists recommend that you take it daily in stressful times.

• Green foods, such as blue-green algae, spirulina, and chlorella, act as antioxidants and are a good source of naturally balanced vitamins, minerals, enzymes, trace elements, and proteins. These can help to boost energy levels and physical and mental performance. Take as directed.

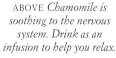
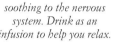

ABOVE *Chamomile is soothing to the nervous system. Drink as an infusion to help you relax.*

WHAT YOU CAN DO TO HELP

♦ Avoid excessive intake of stimulants (such as caffeine) or depressants (alcohol), refined foods, and toxins.

♦ Avoid smoking.

♦ Eat well.

♦ Get enough sleep.

♦ Take time to enjoy life.

♦ Yoga may help to relieve stress and tension, and stretching the body will ease muscle tension and teach you to breathe more efficiently.

♦ Massage and meditation are also excellent relaxation therapies, and can be used in everyday life.

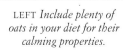

LEFT *Include plenty of oats in your diet for their calming properties.*

Get a Good Night's Sleep

NOT MUCH IS AS *important to our well-being on a day-to-day basis as getting a good night's sleep. Worry is one possible cause of wakefulness, but not the only one. Pain or discomfort, caffeine or alcohol, hunger or overtiredness, lack of fresh air and exercise, can all prevent sleep, or cause you to wake too early.*

Insomnia is considered to be a "primary sleep disorder," which may have either a psychological or physical cause. There are many causes of insomnia, and fortunately almost all can be treated. Most of us will suffer from insomnia at some point in our lives, from one of the following causes:

• The main cause of insomnia is stress or worry; waking in the middle of the night or very early, and being unable to get back to sleep, is a common characteristic of insomnia, which, unfortunately, also becomes more frequent with age.

• Caffeine is a common cause of insomnia, as is alcohol, which may send you off to sleep, but which has a short-lived effect.

• Pain, anxiety, and depression are common causes, as is stress.

• Pregnancy and menopausal symptoms may cause insomnia in some women.

• Spinal problems, especially at the top of the spine, can affect sleep.

BELOW *To insure that you get a good night's sleep, stop working at least an hour before bedtime.*

RIGHT *Back problems, particularly at the top of the spinal column, may impede sleep.*

Other possible causes of insomnia include food allergies, nutritional deficiencies, thyroid disorders, being overtired (you need energy to sleep and to be able to relax properly), lack of fresh air and physical exercise, chronic problems such as skin rashes, digestive disorders, asthma, and catarrh, and acute problems such as infections, toothaches, earaches, coughs, colds, fever, and headaches.

WHAT YOU CAN DO TO HELP

◆ Eat a variety of foods, with plenty of fresh fruit and vegetables.

◆ Avoid sugars, chocolate, cola drinks, tea, and coffee, all of which have toxins that can affect the nervous system and prevent sleep.

◆ Avoid eating just before bedtime.

◆ See a health practitioner if you suffer from any chronic health problems; some complementary health practitioners will be able to treat your health problems as well as any other factors contributing to your insomnia.

◆ Find a means of controlling pain, and learn some relaxation techniques to help you get through the tense hours of early waking.

◆ Stop working at least an hour before bedtime, and try reading something light.

◆ Take more exercise, preferably earlier in the day.

◆ Take a warm (not hot) bath each night before bed, which will have the dual purpose of relaxing you, and also subconsciously "washing away" the problems of the day.

◆ If you cannot get to sleep, switch on the light and read, or do something different, and then go back to sleep.

◆ If you are overtired when you go to bed, try taking a short afternoon nap, to break the cycle.

◆ If possible, remove your clock from your bedroom.

SUPPLEMENTS FOR INSOMNIA

• Eat plenty of food containing calcium, which may encourage sleep. Foods rich in calcium include parsley, dairy produce, broccoli, dried figs, and sesame seeds.

• Suck a zinc lozenge (15mg) just before bedtime, until a sleep pattern is established.

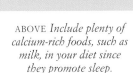

• Insomnia may be caused by a toxic overload, so insure that you drink plenty of water to help your body flush out toxins. Supplements that help the liver to detoxify include B-complex vitamins, digestive enzymes, E.F.A.s, selenium, zinc, magnesium, manganese, taurine (an amino acid), and the antioxidant vitamins. Herbs include turmeric and dandelion root (which stimulate the liver secretions and the flow of bile).

• Take a good B-complex, which aids the nervous system. You'll need 25 to 50mg, twice daily.

• Take a magnesium supplement at 200mg per day. This has been used successfully in the treatment of many types of insomnia.

• Tryptophan, an amino acid, helps to encourage healthy sleep – good sources include avocado, turkey, bananas, or peanut butter.

ABOVE *Include plenty of calcium-rich foods, such as milk, in your diet since they promote sleep.*

RIGHT *Try taking a long, warm bath before bedtime. This will help to make you ready for sleep.*

The Elderly

THE OLDER WE ARE, *the more important it is to eat well and use supplements. Youth can cover misdemeanors in the area of diet in a way that old age cannot. As we age, our bodies' requirements change, and they often become less efficient at assimilating the nutrients in the food we eat. Put simply, age needs more help.*

When the degenerative effects of aging take their toll, a host of chronic and acute health conditions can become part of daily life. But studies show that degeneration – of the mind and the body – can be halted, and sometimes retarted *(see pp. 94–95)*, by using supplements and the tools of nutrition to best effect. To insure our later years are healthy and productive, we need only take care to eat a balanced diet full of antioxidant fruits and vegetables, combined with carefully chosen supplements.

BELOW *Eating garlic will help prevent heart disease and other debilitating aging conditions.*

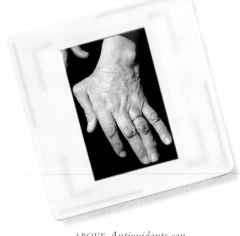

ABOVE *Antioxidants can help prevent degenerative diseases such as arthritis.*

ABOVE *Evening primrose oil, a rich source of essential fatty acids, helps retard the aging process.*

RIGHT *As you get older, try to remain as active as possible and get at least a little exercise every day.*

WHAT YOU CAN DO TO HELP

◆ Eat a good diet, rich in fresh, wholefoods, including at least five servings of fresh fruits and vegetables each day. Most diseases of aging are linked with those who have a low intake of fresh, wholesome foods. Studies show that most elderly people have nutritional deficiencies.

◆ Cut down on fats, and use olive oil, which is the healthiest oil, and is associated with longevity and reduced cholesterol and heart disease.

◆ Insure that your teeth are cared for, and that you have well-fitting dentures if your teeth are not your own. Studies show that poor chewing is a cause of malnutrition in some elderly people.

◆ Remain active. Try to avoid having other people do things for you. Studies show that by continuing to use your body and your brain, you will stay younger for longer. Exercise has a positive effect on both the brain and the body.

◆ If you are suffering from pain in any form, get some complementary treatment. Pain is extremely debilitating and can cause a host of other health problems.

◆ Make sure you have company. Loneliness and depression in old age can lead to self-neglect.

◆ Take measures to boost your immune system *(see pp. 88–89)*.

ABOVE *Ginseng, known as the root of immortality in the East, can be taken in a variety of forms.*

SUPPLEMENTS FOR THE ELDERLY

• Take a good multivitamin and mineral supplement, with extra antioxidants (vitamins A, C, E, and the mineral selenium) to help slow down the aging process. Antioxidants can help to prevent arthritis, cancer, dementia, heart disease, and adult-onset diabetes, as well as extending life expectancy.

• Make sure that you obtain plenty of B vitamins from your food, and take a supplement at 25 to 50mg, twice a day.

• Take an *acidophilus* supplement, and eat plenty of live yogurt, which will help your body to absorb nutrients more effectively.

• Garlic helps to prevent the debilitating effects of aging, and also works to prevent heart disease and

other health conditions associated with aging. Eat plenty of fresh garlic in your diet, or take a supplement, at 500mg daily.

• Take supplements to boost mental agility and memory *(see pp. 98–99)*.

• Take supplements that will help to extend your life *(see pp. 94–95)*.

• Insure that you get plenty of fish oils, and take a fish-oil or evening-primrose oil supplement daily *(see pp. 80–81)*.

BELOW *Live yogurt will help your body to absorb nutrients more effectively.*

Pregnancy

PREGNANCY IS A TIME *when many women become more health-conscious, and during pregnancy it is important to eat well to insure the health and safety of the unborn baby. Research has shown that you need extra folic acid and iron during pregnancy, and, in most cases, during the preconceptual period, and a good multivitamin and mineral supplement is often suggested. Unless prescribed by your physician, it is best to avoid vitamin A supplements, although beta-carotene, an important antioxidant, is safer to use during pregnancy.*

The overuse of supplements when you are pregnant can have a detrimental effect on your unborn baby, but it is sensible to use supplements if your diet is poor, or if you have reason to believe that you are not getting the quantities of vitamins and minerals necessary to insure the health of your baby. If you are not sure about what the safe limits are, see your physician for advice. It is an indisputable fact that the chances of conceiving and giving birth to a healthy baby are increased by a good diet – in both parents. Studies show that diet and environmental factors may be responsible for a much larger proportion of birth defects, stillbirths, and miscarriages than previously believed.

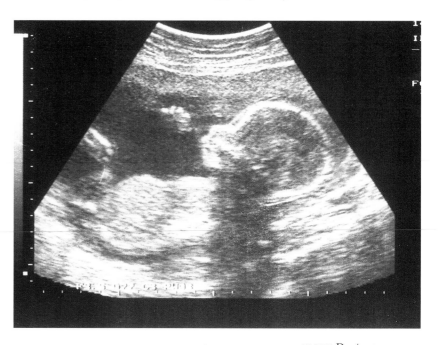

ABOVE D*uring pregnancy there is an increased need for vitamins and minerals to insure both the mother and the baby stay healthy.*

ABOVE *Use supplements carefully during pregnancy and make sure that you follow a good diet.*

LEFT *Avoid charred or barbecued foods during pregnancy because they may harm the unborn baby.*

LEFT *Try to include at least five portions of fresh fruits and vegetables in your daily diet.*

• Take a good multivitamin and mineral tablet with high levels of antioxidants and zinc.

• Avoid taking more than 10,000iu of vitamin A, which can cause birth defects in your unborn baby. Take vitamin A as beta-carotene, which is safer.

• Take a zinc supplement at 10mg per day.

• Take at least 400mcg of folic acid, which will help to prevent birth defects, such as spina bifida.

• Partners should take 1,000mg (1g) of vitamin C daily in the pre-conceptual period (at least six months), and 200iu of vitamin E, as well as extra zinc (up to 25mg daily)

WHAT YOU CAN DO TO HELP

♦ Avoid pollutants and toxins that may cause damage to the unborn baby by interfering with the healthy multiplication of cells. Scientific research has shown that the following can interfere with the conception and birth of a healthy baby: alcohol, tobacco, lead, overheated cooking oil, charred or barbecued foods, radiation, diazepam tranquilizers, paracetamol (acetaminophen), drugs, viruses, infections, and the smoke from diesel engines.

♦ Eat a diet that is rich in wholefoods, and antioxidants, as well as foods that are known to reduce the damage caused by those toxins, or "mutagens," listed above. In her book *The Nutritional Health Bible*, Linda Lazarides writes that foods or ·nutrients that neutralize mutagens (substances capable of causing mutation) include burdock, mint, broccoli, green bell pepper, apples, shallots, pineapples, ginger, cabbage, eggplant, parsley, and grapes. She also points out that the beneficial effects of these seem to be lost when the plants are boiled. Unrefined olive oil and linoleic acid from nuts and seeds may also work against a large number of mutagens.

♦ Avoid taking drugs or medicines, unless prescribed by your physician.

♦ Avoid coffee and caffeine-containing drinks.

♦ Eat five portions of fresh fruits and vegetables each day – organic if you can get them, because organic produce can have up to 100 percent more nutritional value than commercially grown varieties.

♦ Eat whole-wheat breads and cereals, and brown, unpolished rice.

ONLY TAKE DRUGS PRESCRIBED BY YOUR PHYSICIAN

DON'T DRINK TOO MUCH CAFFEINE

TAKE A FOLIC ACID SUPPLEMENT TO HELP PREVENT BIRTH DEFECTS

EAT A DIET RICH IN WHOLEFOODS AND ANTIOXIDANTS

AVOID CHARRED FOODS

LEFT *A healthy diet should be followed by both parents preconceptually and by the mother during pregnancy to insure the well-being of their unborn baby.*

Babies and Children

*BABIES AND CHILDREN have high nutritional requirements, and studies show
that large numbers of school-age children are deficient in many necessary vitamins
and minerals. A poor diet – resulting from faddy or fussy eating – can cause a number
of health problems and lead to behavioral problems, impaired learning, and
an inefficient immune system.*

ABOVE *Children need fat in
their diet, but make sure that
it is healthy fat such as olive
oil or good-quality butter.*

SUPPLEMENTS FOR BABIES AND CHILDREN

• Babies who are breast-fed will not need extra vitamins or minerals, but bottle-fed babies may benefit from vitamin and mineral drops, which can be prescribed by your physician.
• All children can benefit from a good multivitamin and mineral supplement, no matter how good their diet. Any trace deficiencies can be rectified, and studies show that children who have optimum levels of nutrients perform best both academically and athletically, and have normal growth patterns. Insure that there are good levels of the antioxidant vitamins and minerals in your supplement, which can help to maintain healthy organs. Always get advice from your physician before giving supplements to children.

Furthermore, the toxins ingested by many children have a harmful effect on the body and can lead to problems that are not manifested until later life in the form of cancers, immune conditions, heart disease, decreased mental capacity, and emotional and behavioral problems. Parents have an enormous responsibility to insure that their children get a good, healthy diet – a task that is not always easy when faced with fussy eaters.

Children need far lower doses of nutrients than adults, and a healthy and varied organic diet should offer the large proportion of their nutritional needs.

Avoid giving chewable vitamin C tablets between meals, because the acid can eat away at the tooth enamel. Offer chewable vitamin C with meals only.

LEFT *Your child should
have at least one hot
nutritious meal every day.*

WHAT YOU CAN DO TO HELP

◆ If you have a fussy or faddy eater, be patient and consistent and try not to offer fast or convenience foods – which are high in artificial ingredients – as a substitute. Children who become accustomed to the enhanced flavors of commercially prepared foods will find it difficult to be satisfied with blander home cooking.

◆ Insure that your child gets a good, nutritious, hot meal at least once every day.

◆ Children need five servings of fresh fruits and vegetables each day. If vegetables or fruits are unpopular, try grating them and adding them to other dishes, or use a juicer to extract juices and add them to foods and drinks that your child will like. Fresh carrot juice is sweet and delicious, and high in beta-carotene and other nutrients, and most children love the taste. Other vegetables, such as cucumbers and beets, can be added to juices or drunk on their own.

◆ There is no need to cut out fats in a children's diet. Unlike adults, children do need fat. Try to stick to healthy fats, such as olive oil, and use butter instead of margarines.

◆ Offer your child lots of fresh water to drink between meals, which can help the body to work more effectively. Avoid sweet drinks, and drink fruit juices only with food, to reduce the risk of long-term damage to their teeth.

◆ Studies show that many faddy eaters have a zinc deficiency. Increase your child's intake of zinc-rich foods, and ask your pharmacist for a specially prepared zinc supplement for children (usually sucked).

◆ Try to breast-feed your baby. Breast milk is designed to provide complete nourishment for a baby for several months after its birth. Before milk is produced the mother's breast produces colostrum, a deep-yellow liquid containing high levels of protein and antibodies. A newborn baby who feeds on colostrum in the first few days of life is better able later to resist the bacteria and viruses that cause illness. The mother's milk, which begins to flow a few days after childbirth when the mother's hormones change, is a blue-white color with a very thin consistency. If the mother is well nourished, the milk provides the baby with the complete balance of nutrition. The fat contained in human milk, compared with cow's milk, is more digestible for infants and allows for greater absorption of fat-soluble vitamins into the bloodstream from the baby's intestine.

◆ Calcium and other important nutrients in human milk are also better utilized by infants. Antigens in cow's milk can cause allergic reactions in a newborn child, whereas such reactions to human milk are rare. Human milk also promotes growth, largely due to the presence of certain hormones and growth factors. Breast-fed babies have a very low risk of developing meningitis or severe blood infections, and have a 500 to 600 percent lower risk of getting childhood lymphoma. Breast-fed babies also suffer 50 percent fewer middle-ear infections.

BELOW *Breast milk is best for babies. It contains all the nutrients that a newborn baby requires.*

Women

WOMEN HAVE CLEARLY *defined nutritional needs that change as they age and pass through various cycles. Many women are deficient in a number of vitamins and minerals, partly through following low-calorie or "fad" diets to lose weight, and partly because of the stress of trying to juggle, in many cases, a family, a job, and a home.*

Women who take the contraceptive pill will require different supplements than women who are experiencing the menopause. Breast-feeding and pregnant women both have massive nutritional requirements *(see pp. 106–107)*, and menstruating women are different again. You will need to take time to figure out your exact nutritional needs before embarking on a program of supplementation, and some of the information listed opposite may help.

MANY WOMEN FOLLOW A LOW-CALORIE DIET

ABOVE *Dried fruits are a good source of iron and may help women with heavy menstrual periods.*

WORKING MOTHERS CAN FIND IT DIFFICULT TO COPE WITH THEIR DUAL ROLE

YOUNG CHILDREN CAN BE DEMANDING

ABOVE *Your nutritional needs will change if you take the contraceptive pill.*

LEFT *Women often suffer from nutritional deficiency due to the stress of work and home life.*

SUPPLEMENTS FOR WOMEN

Many of the following vitamins and minerals can be taken as part of a good multivitamin and mineral supplement, and the dosages listed provide guidance for the levels you should expect to receive from your maintenance-level supplement on a daily basis. Where your overall supplement falls short, you may wish to try individual vitamins or minerals. For specific health conditions, refer to the the Self-help for Illnesses section *(see pp. 114–139)*. To improve overall health, extend your life, and boost your immunity, refer to Supplements for All-round Good Health *(see pp. 86–113)*.

• Women need between 5,000 and 25,000iu of vitamin A as beta-carotene daily. Women who are planning a pregnancy or who are pregnant, should not take vitamin A (retinol) in excess of 10,000iu daily.
• The B-complex vitamins should be taken three times daily, at between 10 and 25mg. Vitamin B3 should be taken at 10 to 200mg.
• Vitamin C is required at between 200 and 600mg daily, broken into three doses.
• Women need between 200 and 400iu of vitamin D, taken as ergocalciferol (vitamin D2).
• Women should have 200 to 400iu of vitamin E.
• Women with a heavy monthly blood loss may need an iron supplement, particularly if they are fitted with an intrauterine device (I.U.D.). The best form of iron is found in meat, and should be taken by itself or with vitamin C for maximum absorption. Other good sources are dried fruits and green leafy vegetables. Take 10 to 15mg daily as a supplement.

• Iodine, obtained from kelp or as potassium iodide, is required at 75 to 150mcg daily.
• Zinc, as zinc gluconate or picolinate, should be taken at 10 to 15mg daily.
• Selenium, an antioxidant, at 50 to 200mcg.
• Molybdenum, at 50 to 100mcg.
• Calcium, at 200 to 1,000mg.
• Copper, at 1 to 2mg.
• Chromium, at 50 to 200mcg daily.
• Magnesium, at 200 to 400mg.
• Manganese, at 5 to 10mg.
• Women with P.M.S. should increase their intake of vitamin B6 up to 25mg daily, and take an evening primrose capsule *(see p. 136)*. Take chromium at 200mcg daily, and add fish oils, at 2,000 to 3,000mg per day.
• Postmenopausal women will need extra antioxidants, as well as increased calcium (600 to 1,200mg per day). Take 3mg of boron, which helps to prevent the bone-wasting disease, osteoporosis.

• Pregnant and breast-feeding women have different needs *(see pp.106–107)*.
• Ginseng will help to increase energy levels and tonify the body, and is particularly useful for women suffering from stress.
• Agnus castus is useful for women with P.M.S. and menopause symptoms, and should be taken as a tincture (25 drops, three times daily) or as a daily tablet. This herb helps to regulate hormone levels.
• Garlic, either eaten fresh on a daily basis, or taken as a supplement, will help to insure cardiac health.

BELOW *Postmenopausal women should consider taking a daily multiformula tailored to this phase of life.*

A supplement formulated for postmenopausal women will contain extra calcium and antioxidants.

Men

MEN ARE LESS LIKELY *than women to pay attention to their well-being, especially how it can be affected or improved by diet and lifestyle. According to recent research, men still drink and smoke more than women, although the gap is narrowing. This combination of factors mean that the overall health of many men is well below optimum level. Fortunately, there are many ways in which these health issues can be addressed.*

ABOVE *Men generally lead a far more unhealthy lifestyle than women, which leads to all kinds of health problems in later life.*

ABOVE *Men should take a daily supplement of garlic to help prevent the onset of coronary disease.*

Studies show that men are much less interested in their nutritional status than women and are far less likely to supplement in order to meet their nutritional needs. Increased stress levels in our modern society have caused a huge number of nutritional deficiencies that need to be met with supplements and/or an improved diet. Furthermore, a huge range of health conditions specific to men can be treated using the elements of nutrition. The daily needs of men are similar to those of women, and men will benefit from taking a daily supplement with the same nutritional content as that listed for women *(see pp. 110–111).* Men still generally drink more alcohol and smoke more than women, so they will need to take extra vitamins and minerals to help prevent long-term damage to their bodies.

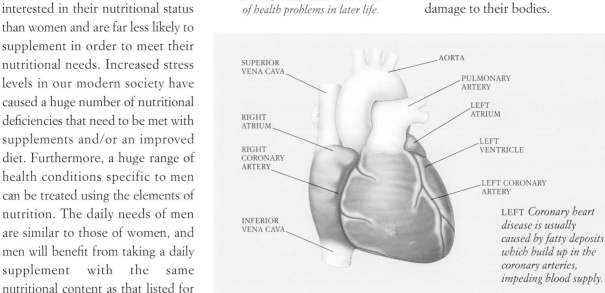

SUPERIOR VENA CAVA

AORTA

PULMONARY ARTERY

LEFT ATRIUM

RIGHT ATRIUM

LEFT VENTRICLE

RIGHT CORONARY ARTERY

LEFT CORONARY ARTERY

INFERIOR VENA CAVA

LEFT *Coronary heart disease is usually caused by fatty deposits which build up in the coronary arteries, impeding blood supply.*

SUPPLEMENTS FOR MEN

• Many of the following vitamins and minerals can be taken as part of a good multivitamin and mineral supplement, and the dosages listed provide guidance for the levels you should expect to receive from your maintenance-level supplement on a daily basis. Where your overall supplement falls short, you may wish to try individual vitamins or minerals. For specific health conditions, refer to the the Self-help for Illnesses section (*see pp. 114–139*). To improve overall health, extend your life, and boost your immunity, refer to Supplements for All-round Good Health (*see pp. 86–113*).

• Men need to take between 5,000 and 25,000iu of vitamin A as beta-carotene.
• The B-complex vitamins should be taken three times daily, at between 10 and 25mg. Vitamin B3 should be taken at 10 to 200mg.
• Vitamin C is required at between 200 and 600mg daily, broken into three doses.
• Men need between 200 and 400iu of vitamin D, taken as ergocalciferol (vitamin D2).
• Take 250mg of fish oil daily.
• Men need to take 200 to 400iu of vitamin E.
• Iodine, from kelp, or as potassium iodide, is required by men at 75 to 150mcg daily.
• Zinc, as zinc gluconate or picolinate, should be taken at 10 to 15mg daily.
• Take selenium, an antioxidant, at 50 to 200mcg.
• Molybdenum, at 50 to 100mcg.
• Calcium, at 200 to 1,000mg
• Copper, at 1 to 2mg.

• Chromium, at 50 to 200mcg.
• Magnesium, at 200 to 400mg.
• Manganese, at 5 to 10mg.
• Men suffering from prostate enlargement should take extra vitamin B-complex, up to 50mg daily, with 15 to 20mg of zinc.
• Men with a reduced sperm count will benefit from extra vitamin C (1,000mg spread over three doses on a daily basis). They should also take extra zinc (15 to 20mg daily).

• If you suffer from stress take extra supplements (*see pp. 100–101*).
• Men who are athletic will need extra magnesium, at 200mg per day, and a good antioxidant preparation.
• Because heart disease is still more common in men, supplements to insure a healthy heart will be useful. It is recommended that all men take a garlic supplement daily, and get plenty of antioxidants, which can help to prevent oxidative damage to the heart.

BELOW *Many men take poor care of their health and may need supplements to insure their well-being.*

ATHLETIC MEN NEED MAGNESIUM

GARLIC HELPS PREVENT HEART DISEASE

TAKE ANTIOXIDANTS IF YOU PLAY A LOT OF SPORTS

B-COMPLEX WILL HELP PROSTATE DISORDERS

VITAMIN C AND ZINC HELP WITH LOW SPERM COUNT

Self-Help for Illnesses

WE NOW KNOW THAT *nutritional deficiencies cause many chronic illnesses and are responsible for an increased susceptibility to acute conditions. Ideally, healthy eating should provide adequate quantities of most vitamins, minerals, and other elements of nutrition, but many of us still suffer from health conditions that are specifically linked to deficiency, however slight. Fortunately, supplements are available to redress these deficiencies and imbalances.*

The first step is to eat a varied, balanced diet, rich in the vitamins and minerals that are outlined in preceding pages of this book. The second step is to take a good "insurance-level" multi-vitamin and mineral supplement. The third step, and here this section will help you, is to perhaps add to your diet any nutrients that may have a therapeutic use for a particular condition from which you are suffering. For the dosages of individual nutrients, follow the advice in the Listings section, unless a dose is suggested here.

If you suffer from any long-term illnesses or are on medication, it is best to seek advice from a professional. If you are confused about taking a number of different supplements, expert advice may also be necessary *(see pp. 24–25)*. Remember that each individual has different requirements, and what may balance and work therapeutically for one person, may unbalance and cause problems in another person.

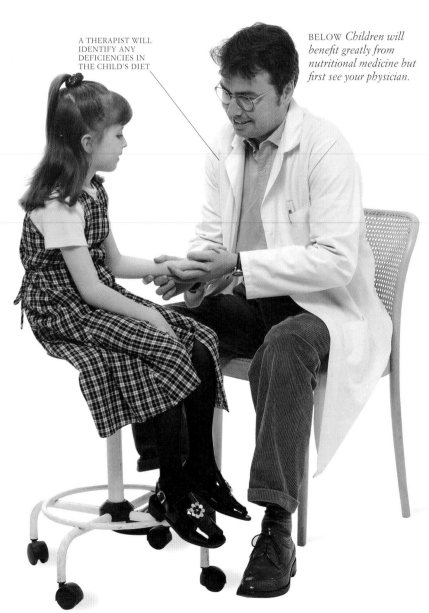

A THERAPIST WILL IDENTIFY ANY DEFICIENCIES IN THE CHILD'S DIET

BELOW *Children will benefit greatly from nutritional medicine but first see your physician.*

BROCCOLI

RICE

LEFT *A balanced diet should give you all the nutrients that you require.*

WHITE FISH

CARROT CAKE

TIPS FOR CHOOSING SUPPLEMENTS

There are a few tips to bear in mind when you are choosing which supplements to take:

• Avoid taking any one vitamin or mineral in large quantities, unless you are under the supervision of a physician or nutrition specialist. The balance of vitamins, minerals, and other elements in your body can be upset and more harm can be done than good.

• Experiment with one substance before you begin to combine them. Taking a specific herb or nutrient for a week to 10 days will help you to identify any possible problems, and gage its effect on your body, your mind, your energy levels, and your emotions. You'll also be able to see what substances may cause an allergy, or other adverse reaction.

• Many vitamins and minerals, and herbs and other substances, work well in combination. Investigate your local health store or pharmacy to see the range of combination remedies – it may save you time in trying to combine your own.

• A good multivitamin and mineral supplement should cover all your needs, unless you are suffering from a specific condition that may warrant the use of particular nutrients.

• Eat a balanced diet and remember that supplements are not a replacement for food.

• Take supplements regularly throughout the day, and with food *(see p. 21 for exceptions).*

• Extra doses of specific nutrients should not need to be taken for longer than four to six weeks, unless there are special circumstances. You should begin to see results within two to three weeks of beginning supplementation. If not, chances are that it is not doing any good.

SAFETY

It is important to exercise caution when taking any supplements. If you are pregnant, breast-feeding, taking medication, or suffer from a chronic health condition, you are advised to discuss any supplementation with your physician before beginning. Children respond very well to nutritional medicine, but again, talk to your physician before altering a child's diet, or offering supplements. If you have concerns about the safety of any supplement, see your physician or registered therapist. Always pay close attention to potency, dosage level, frequency of use, and your body size. The higher the potency and the dosage level, the more likely it is that a herb or nutritional substance can have drug-like effects.

The supplement levels suggested throughout this book are safe and nontoxic for the vast majority of adults. If you suspect a herb or nutritional substance is causing an adverse reaction, stop using it and try something that is better suited to your body and its needs.

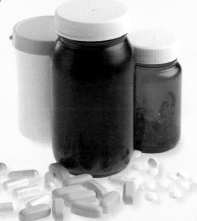

RIGHT *Always exercise caution when taking supplements and follow instructions carefully.*

115

Skin

ALTHOUGH IT HAS *great protective qualities and is resistant to most of the insults that our daily lives throw at it, the skin can be a very sensitive barometer of imbalances within us. The lower layers of the skin are made up of living cells, and changes in the levels of various essential nutrients can lead to a wide range of skin conditions, including dryness, soreness, and both viral and bacterial infections.*

ACNE

Acne is caused by the over-production of sebum, an oily substance that causes the pores of the skin to become blocked, resulting in spots or pimples. Acne is particularly common among adolescents due to hormonal changes.

• Nutritionists believe that acne may be caused by deficiencies of vitamin A, vitamin B6, essential fatty acids, zinc, and/or vitamin E. Factors associated with acne include food allergies and intolerances, a sluggish liver, a high-fat diet, hormones, and the contraceptive pill.

• Eat as many fresh fruits and vegetables as possible, preferably raw, and reduce your intake of wheat and fatty foods.
• Take a zinc supplement (30mg every day).
• B6 supplementation is useful for cases of premenstrual acne.
• Take a good antioxidant that includes vitamins A, C, and E, along with selenium, lack of which has been linked to some cases of acne.

PSORIASIS

Psoriasis is a noncontagious skin disease that commonly affects the knees, elbows, and scalp, but may also occur on the hands and feet. Bright pink, raised patches, covered with white scales appear on the skin. When psoriasis occurs on the hands or feet pustules may form. The complaint is caused by overproduction of epidermal cells and may be triggered by stress.

• Some cases of psoriasis are caused or exacerbated by heavy alcohol consumption, deficiencies of fresh fruits and vegetables in the diet, nutritional deficiencies, and a sluggish liver. Deficiencies of folic acid, selenium, and possibly zinc and calcium can occur, particularly if the condition is widespread.
• Increase your intake of essential fatty acids, particularly omega-3, which is known to help psoriasis.
• Increase your intake of fish oils, or take a daily supplement of four to six tablets.
• Avoid wheat, oats, barley, and rye, to which you may have a sensitivity.
• Take a good multivitamin and mineral supplement, with extra zinc (30mg per day), selenium (50mcg per day), and vitamin E, in dry form (400iu, three times daily).

BELOW *If you suffer from skin conditions, try increasing your intake of fresh fruits.*

BANANA

WHITE GRAPES

ORANGE

BLACK GRAPES

PEAR

COLD SORES

Cold sores are caused by the herpes simplex virus. These painful pus-filled blisters usually appear around the mouth. The virus may lie dormant in the body and only flares up when the immune system is under stress. Cold sores are very contagious and care should be taken not to spread them to other parts of the body or to other people.

• Cold sores are usually precipitated by stress, fatigue, a poor diet (even short term), illness, and, in some women, premenstrually.
• Increasing your intake of vitamin C and garlic will encourage immunity and prevent attacks.
• Zinc will help to promote healing.
• Take a good vitamin and mineral supplement, and take extra *acidophilus* or eat plenty of live yogurt, to encourage growth of the body's "healthy" bacteria, or flora.
• L-lysine is effective in treating cold sores.

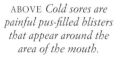

ABOVE *Cold sores are painful pus-filled blisters that appear around the area of the mouth.*

RIGHT *If you suffer from cold sores, take more vitamin C, which can be found in citrus fruits.*

ECZEMA

Eczema is an inflamed and itchy skin condition. The skin often becomes red, flaky, and may also have tiny blisters leading to weepy sores and scabs. There are many types of eczema including contact eczema (caused by hypersensitivity to an allergen such as a detergent) and atopic eczema (associated with allergies such as hay fever). Eczema may also flare up as a result of prolonged stress.
• Some of the most common causes of eczema include allergies, to foods, and to substances, an essential fatty acid (E.F.A.) deficiency, and a zinc deficiency.

• Experts suggest that you alter your diet to cut out specific foods that may be causing or exacerbating the problem, including citrus fruits, cow's milk, eggs, wheat, and artificial colorings.
• Use nonbiological laundry detergent, and wear cotton or another natural-fiber clothing.
• Take extra B-complex vitamins and zinc (at 30mg per day of each), as well as E.F.A.s. Fish oils and evening primrose have been shown in studies to reduce itching, and improve the condition in a large percentage of sufferers.

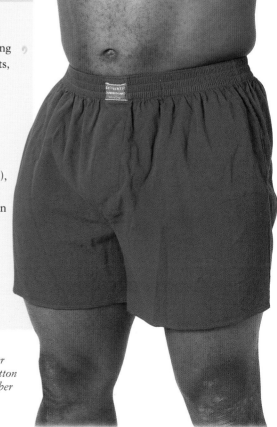

RIGHT *If you suffer from eczema, wear cotton or another natural fiber next to your skin.*

Breathing

FOR EFFICIENT, EASY *breathing the whole of the respiratory system must be clear and open from the nose and sinuses to the tiny alveoli or air sacs, deep in the lungs. Viral infections, allergic reactions, and other respiratory diseases can tend to restrict the passage of air by causing tissues to swell and fluid to build up in the nasal passages, major airways, and the lungs.*

ASTHMA

The main symptoms of asthma are breathlessness, wheeziness, and tightness in the chest. During an asthmatic attack the bronchial tubes become partially obstructed making breathing difficult. Attacks may be triggered by an allergen such as pollen or fur, infections of the respiratory tract, strenuous exercise, or anxiety. Asthma generally starts in childhood and will often disappear by puberty.

• Some of the nutritional causes of asthma are believed to be food allergies or intolerances, magnesium deficiency, pollution, and selenium and vitamin B6 deficiency.
• Do not smoke, and avoid pollutants and damp.
• Onions are believed to have antiasthmatic properties, and it is suggested that you have at least one onion, cooked, each day.

• Vitamin C should be taken at 1g, twice each day, for its antihistamine activity.
• Magnesium is believed to dilate the bronchial tubes, preventing spasm, and it works to encourage a normal response to allergens. A daily supplement of 300 to 400mg is recommended.
• Vitamin B6 was shown to reduce the number of asthma attacks in a group of patients studied in 1985.
• Antioxidants vitamin A (as beta-carotene), C, and E, as well as selenium, should encourage recovery and prevent attacks.
• Gingko biloba has been used for thousands of years to treat asthma and allergies. Take 60mg per day.

RIGHT *If you suffer from asthma, it is recommended that you eat at least one cooked onion every day.*

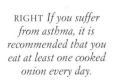

BRONCHITIS

Bronchitis indicates an inflammation of the mucous lining of the main air passages of the lungs. Its symptoms include coughing that produces sputum, breathlessness, wheeziness, and chest pain. Acute bronchitis starts with a respiratory infection and usually clears up within a few days. Chronic bronchitis, however, is a serious, long-term condition primarily caused by smoking.

• Chronic bronchitis has a number of nutritional causes, including smoking (which robs the body of essential vitamins and minerals, as well as damaging the lungs, and introducing toxins and carcinogenic substances to the body), pollution, and deficiencies of vitamin C and zinc.
• It is suggested that 1g of vitamin C be taken twice daily, for a four-to eight-week period, to encourage healing, boost the immune response, and act as a natural antihistamine.
• Take 30mg of zinc daily.
• If you smoke, insure that you get extra vitamin C and B-complex, and make sure you take a good antioxidant supplement. Best of all, try to quit.

COMMON COLD AND FLU

The common cold is caused by a number of different viruses. The symptoms include sneezing, a sore throat, coughing, and a runny nose. Flu is also caused by a virus and normally occurs in epidemics. It is characterized by fever, aching muscles, sore throat, and a headache. The fever subsides after a few days, leaving the sufferer feeling weak and lacking in energy.

• The common cold and flu are caused by a huge number of viruses, and if you are run down, you are more likely to be susceptible.

• Vitamins A and C, and zinc, can help to prevent colds and flu, and during the cold season, it is recommended that you take double the recommended dose of each, to help prevent infection.

• If you have a cold or flu, take 1g of vitamin C, three times daily, and suck a zinc lozenge every two hours, up to six times a daily.

• Echinacea should be taken two to three times daily, to boost the immune system. About 25 drops of tincture (half that for children) should be taken each time.

• Garlic capsules or fresh garlic should be taken each day.

• Drink plenty of fresh water to flush the system, and drink hot water with lemon juice to cleanse your respiratory system.

LEMONS AND HOT WATER

ABOVE *Drink an infusion of hot water and lemons to help cleanse your respiratory system. Be sure to allow the water to cool slightly – boiling water will destroy the vitamin C to some extent.*

RIGHT *The symptoms of the common cold include sneezing and a runny nose.*

LEFT *Smoking can severely damage the respiratory system. Quit to prevent long-term damage.*

Immune System

YOUR BODY RELIES *on the immune system to react quickly and correctly in order to combat disease-causing viruses and bacteria. If the immune response is impaired for any reason, the body can easily become overwhelmed by infections or infestations that it would normally fight off with ease. In many cases, dietary remedies can help to improve the function of the immune system and encourage healing.*

H.I.V. AND A.I.D.S.

H.I.V. (human immunodeficiency virus) weakens the immune system, leaving it susceptible to opportunistic infections. It can be contracted through unsafe sex, contaminated blood, breast-feeding, or at birth from an infected mother. Once present in the body, H.I.V. remains for life, and may eventually lead to A.I.D.S.

• A.I.D.S., or Acquired Immune Deficiency Syndrome, responds well to nutritional therapy, and treatment would be aimed at boosting the immune response. People who are H.I.V.-positive will benefit from these remedies, and studies show that a good diet, with extra supplementation, can help to delay the onset of A.I.D.S.
• Selenium deficiency is common among A.I.D.S. patients, and it is suggested that selenium is included as part of a good antioxidant supplement.

• The herb echinacea will help to boost immune activity, as well as acting as a natural antibiotic.
• Increase your intake of live yogurt, or take an *acidophilus* supplement to encourage growth of natural healthy bacteria (flora), which will help to fight off invaders.
• Coenzyme Q10 deficiency is believed to be one of the causative factors of A.I.D.S., and it is recommended that you take a daily dose supplement (200mg).
• Magnesium and vitamin A, as well as vitamin C, will help to ease symptoms and may halt the development of the disease.

ALLERGIES

The immune system protects the body from harmful microbes by producing antibodies that kill the invading organism. However, sometimes the body overreacts and responds in the same way to harmless substances and produces an irritant substance known as histamine, which results in an allergic reaction.

• There may be a genetic predisposition to allergies.
• Zinc and copper are believed to be deficient in many sufferers and should be supplemented as part of a good vitamin and mineral supplement, especially in children.
• Magnesium deficiency can alter the immune response, and it is suggested that you take a supplement, or increase your intake of magnesium-rich foods.
• Vitamin C and bioflavonoids should be taken daily.
• Vitamin E is a good stimulant for the immune system.
• Drink plenty of fresh water and fresh lemon juice to cleanse the system, and eat fresh fruit and vegetables, which will help the body to detoxify.
• Gingko biloba has been used for thousands of years to treat asthma and allergies. Take 60mg per day.

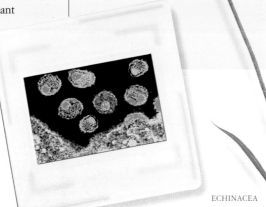

FAR RIGHT *Echinacea is one of the best immune stimulants and is effective in fighting infections.*

RIGHT *The H.I.V. virus weakens the immune system leaving it susceptible to infection.*

ECHINACEA

CHRONIC FATIGUE SYNDROME AND M.E. (MYALGIC ENCEPHALOMYELITIS)

Chronic fatigue syndrome and M.E. can be seriously debilitating complaints and may affect a person for years. Symptoms include depression, extreme tiredness, muscle fatigue, memory lapses, and pain. It is thought that a deficiency in the immune system may be responsible for these diseases.

• M.E. is, in fact, a type of chronic fatigue syndrome, and both may have nutritional causes, including a Candida infestation, food allergies and intolerances, a toxic overload, and nutritional deficiencies.

• Take an *acidophilus* supplement, or eat plenty of live yogurt (live sheep's yogurt is good if you suspect a dairy-food allergy) to increase your body's natural healthy bacteria. This will help to counter Candida infestation.

• Ginseng will help to boost the immune system and to increase energy levels. It will also enhance mental performance.

• Make sure you get plenty of magnesium, which can affect the immune response, and which may be deficient in sufferers.

• Vitamins A, C, and E, and the mineral zinc, as well as E.F.A.s and fish oils, have been used successfully to treat sufferers of chronic fatigue. Most of these substances have a beneficial effect on the immune system.

• Eat wholesome food often, and in small quantities. Try to cut down on sugary foods and refined carbo-hydrate.

• Fresh fruits and vegetables should be eaten as often as possible, preferably raw, to help the body detoxify.

• Drink plenty of fresh water with fresh lemon juice to cleanse.

• Echinacea has been used in many cases to boost immune activity; take for three weeks on, and one week off, at normal dosage while the condition persists.

MONONUCLEOSIS (GLANDULAR FEVER)

The early symptoms of mononucleosis are similar to those of flu – fever, headache, sore throat. After a few days the glands in the neck, armpits, and groin will become swollen. Full recovery is slow.

• The causative agent is Epstein-Barr virus (E.B.V.), a herpes virus.

• Supplementing the amino acid L-lysine will encourage healing and reduce the severity of the infection.

• Selenium works to protect the integrity of cell membranes, which improves their overall function.

• Royal jelly and bee pollen are excellent immune boosters.

• Spirulina and chlorella boost immunity and can be taken daily.

• Vitamins A and C work to encourage immune activity.

• Take echinacea and garlic to boost the immune system.

• Take zinc up to 6 times daily.

HODGKIN'S DISEASE

Hodgkin's disease is a form of lymphoma, a cancer that affects the lymphatic tissue and other tissues important in fighting infection. Early symptoms include fever, lymph node enlargement, and weight loss. In later stages of the disease the nodes become rubbery and the spleen and liver become enlarged. The cause is unknown, but viral and other infectious agents, as well as abnormalities of the immune system, have been suggested.

• Eat as much fresh fruit and vegetables as you can, particularly those containing the antioxidants.

• A deficiency of vitamin C has been linked with certain tumors. Insure you get plenty in your diet.

• Vitamin A can protect against cancer to some degree, particularly in smokers.

• Digestive enzymes may be offered to halt the activities of trophoblastic cancer cells.

• Vitamin E is said to prevent a number of cancers; insure that you get plenty in your diet or take supplements.

BELOW *Drink plenty of liquids. Make fresh juices from immune-enhancing vegetables such as carrot.*

Circulatory System

ONE OF THE BODY'S *main systems, the circulatory system, performs a host of essential tasks. These include carrying oxygen from the lungs to all parts of the body and taking carbon dioxide back to the lungs, transporting nutrients and waste materials around the body. Many elements in the circulatory system can benefit from supplements.*

ANEMIA

Anemia is caused by a deficiency of hemoglobin in the blood. There are a number of nutritional deficiencies that cause anemia, including too little iron, vitamin B12, or folic acid. Genetic defects such as sickle-cell anemia may also produce faulty hemoglobin. The characteristic symptoms of anemia include breathlessness, pale skin, dizziness, tiredness, fainting, and palpitations.

• The main causes of anemia are nutritional deficiencies of iron in particular, but also folic acid and vitamin B12. It may be exacerbated by blood loss, from heavy periods, or bleeding from the bowel. Poor absorption of nutrients may also cause the condition.
• Take supplemental iron, as prescribed by your physician (usually about 200mg per day), along with vitamin C, which will double its absorption.
• Vitamin B12 deficiency should be righted with normal doses, and then folic acid may be added thereafter (not together).
• Also take 100mg of vitamin C with each meal, along with 10mg zinc and 1mg copper.
• Take an *acidophilus* tablet, or eat plenty of live yogurt, to encourage growth of healthy bacteria in the bowel that will help you to absorb nutrients more efficiently.

HIGH BLOOD PRESSURE

As the blood flows around the body it exerts pressure on the arterial wall; hypertension, or high blood pressure, occurs when this pressure is above normal level. This puts the circulatory system under considerable strain and may result in stroke or heart failure if left untreated. The condition is often symptomless and is often only diagnosed during a routine blood pressure check.

• High blood pressure may be caused by deficiencies of essential fatty acids (E.F.A.s), as well as calcium and magnesium. Hypertension (high blood pressure) has been commonly associated with a low intake of magnesium.
• Magnesium can be taken daily at between 200 and 300mg to help lower blood pressure, and to improve the balance of potassium, which is often reduced in hypertension (high blood pressure). Potassium should not be supplemented, but it is suggested that you eat plenty of fresh fruits and vegetables daily to get adequate amounts. Potassium antagonizes salt (sodium), which can cause and exacerbate the condition.
• Calcium may have a role in lowering blood pressure, and should be taken daily at between 500 and 1,000mg.
• Fish-oil supplements have also been proven to lower blood pressure in recent studies, and four capsules should be taken daily.
• Get plenty of exercise, and if you are overweight, take steps to lose it – excess body weight is associated with high blood pressure.
• Garlic can have a positive effect on blood pressure. It can be eaten fresh daily, or may be taken in capsule form.
• Coenzyme Q10 has now been shown to improve hypertension by reducing both systolic and diastolic pressure. It has a beneficial effect on the function of the walls of the blood vessels, and it should be taken at doses of between 120 and 360mg per day.

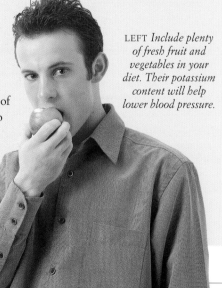

LEFT *Include plenty of fresh fruit and vegetables in your diet. Their potassium content will help lower blood pressure.*

HEART DISEASE

Coronary heart disease is·one of the main causes of premature death in developed countries, such as the United States. The disease occurs when fatty deposits (atheroma) build up on the walls of the coronary arteries leading to atherosclerosis, a narrowing of the arteries. Many factors have been identified by medical researchers as contributing risks, including lack of exercise, a high-fat diet, smoking, high blood pressure, genetic makeup, and stress.

• A huge number of supplements and nutrients can be taken to prevent and treat heart disease, and only some of them have been considered here.
• Garlic has been shown to lower cholesterol levels, and to improve blood pressure and the stickiness of platelets. It also has antioxidant properties, which can significantly reduce the susceptibility of fats in the blood to oxidation (oxidation can have a negative effect on heart function). For best effect, take 600 to 1,000mg of pure or concentrated garlic each day.
• Studies show that diets lacking in E.F.A.s are characterized by elevated cholesterol levels, and increased platelet stickiness. E.F.A.s will also help to reduce blood pressure, and will help to widen the blood vessels. The best dose is 500 to 1,000mg per day, in the form of fish oils.
• Ginger is said to help reduce cholesterol levels, and it may reduce platelet stickiness and prevent clots.
• Ginseng is believed to have a healthy effect on cholesterol levels and platelets; in some people it lowers blood pressure, although it may cause a rise in others.
• Magnesium (at 450 to 650mg per day) and vitamin B6 (as part of a B-complex supplement) may help to reduce the likelihood of clots.

• Vitamin C is thought to lower total cholesterol levels, and it may have a beneficial effect on blood pressure. The antioxidant properties of vitamin C will help to encourage overall health of the heart.
• Coenzyme Q10 has been used successfully in the treatment and prevention of angina, arrhythmia, and other types of heart disease. It is also an essential nutrient for the heart, and an antioxidant, and can help the cells produce energy to keep the heart beating. Doses can range from 15 to 100mg per day used therapeutically and preventively.
• Vitamin E can reduce platelet stickiness and reduce the risk of heart disease. Take 400 to 600iu daily, but seek advice if you have been prescribed "blood-thinning" drugs.
• Chromium has also been linked with lower rates of heart disease, and supplements can be taken at 200 to 400mcg daily to help prevent any coronary dysfunction.
• Fiber also helps to prevent heart disease, and levels in the diet should be increased.

RAYNAUD'S DISEASE

Raynaud's disease is a complaint in which the arteries of the fingers or toes go into spasm when exposed to the cold. There may be a tingling, burning, or numb sensation in the fingers or toes. The affected areas turn white, then blue, then red. This disorder affects mainly young women.

• Studies show that Raynaud's disease may be caused in part by E.F.A. (essential fatty acid) deficiency, and possibly a magnesium deficiency.
• Magnesium supplements are believed to reduce the tendency of blood vessels to spasm, and can be taken at about 450mg per day.
• Fish-oil supplements (four to six capsules per day) and plenty of oily fish in the diet should help.
• Vitamin B3 as nicotinic acid, up to 300mg per day in three doses taken with food, may be useful.

ABOVE *Regular exercise will reduce the risk of heart disease.*

Digestive and Urinary Systems

THE DIGESTIVE SYSTEM *processes everything we eat and drink to supply the body with the energy and material that it needs to function, and build and maintain itself. It comprises the digestive tract from the mouth through the stomach, small and large intestines, to the anus. The urinary system filters and excretes waste material from the bloodstream.*

CROHN'S DISEASE

Crohn's disease causes part of the digestive tract to become inflamed. Symptoms include abdominal pain, diarrhea, weight loss, and poor appetite. The cause is not known.

• Many Crohn's sufferers have an above-average level of sugar in their diet, which may be causing, or exacerbating, the condition. There is also evidence that the increased permeability of the gut causes nutrients to be inadequately absorbed, which means that higher quantities are required. Food allergies and intolerance may also contribute to the condition, and some believe that the immune system has become overactive.
• Nutrients to boost and balance immune activity include selenium, royal jelly, zinc, and vitamins A, C, and E.
• Where there is severe diarrhea, always take soluble supplements, which have a better chance of being absorbed before they reach the gut.
• Iron may be required if there is heavy blood loss, and if you are taking antibiotics, insure that you eat plenty of live yogurt, or take a daily *acidophilus* tablet.
• Selenium is particularly useful where diet is restricted, and severe or long-standing conditions should respond to vitamin A.

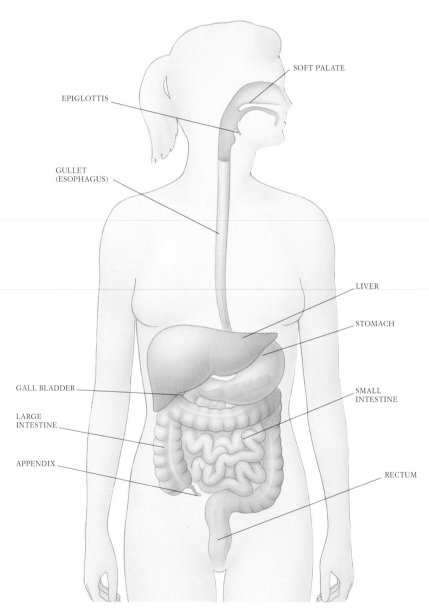

SOFT PALATE

EPIGLOTTIS

GULLET
(ESOPHAGUS)

LIVER

STOMACH

GALL BLADDER

SMALL
INTESTINE

LARGE
INTESTINE

APPENDIX

RECTUM

ABOVE *The digestive system is designed to take in and process food to provide the raw materials the body needs to maintain itself and function properly.*

HEMORRHOIDS (PILES)

Hemorrhoids or piles are varicose veins in the lower part of the rectum or anus. The veins become swollen because of increased pressure, often as a result of constipation and straining during defecation. They are common during pregnancy or if a person is overweight. Occasionally they protrude outside the anus, and are known as prolapsed hemorrhoids.

• Most cases of hemorrhoids are caused by constipation, which responds well to nutritional medicine.
• Magnesium is likely to be deficient, since it is required for the control of the smooth muscles of the body, of which the lining of the gut is one type. When magnesium is low, the muscle groups do not contract and relax in their usual sequence.

• Insure that your diet is rich in fiber, especially in the form of oats, which hold a lot of water and stimulate bowel movements. Take a fiber supplement, such as linseeds.
• Insure that you get plenty to drink. Fresh water or diluted fruit juices are particularly good because they will soften the stool.
• Garlic and onions will also work to soften the stool, and help to cleanse the system. Insure that you get plenty in your diet.
• Rub a little vitamin E oil around the anus, with your finger, to encourage external healing.
• Bioflavonoids and vitamin C will help to insure the integrity of the blood vessels, which makes hemorrhoids less likely.

ABOVE *If you have hemorrhoids, drink plenty of diluted fruit juices to help soften your stools.*

IRRITABLE BOWEL SYNDROME (I.B.S.)

Irritable bowel syndrome is characterized by alternating bouts of diarrhea and constipation, abdominal pain, and wind. Many people also have a feeling of general tiredness and malaise. I.B.S. can be triggered by stress, food intolerance, and insufficient dietary fiber.

• Some of the most common causes of irritable bowel syndrome are constipation and food allergies or intolerance, and in many sufferers there is an infestation of Candida, which makes the condition worse.
• Drink plenty of purified or bottled water, at least six or eight glasses a day, but don't drink with meals, which can dilute stomach acids.

• Make sure you get adequate soluble fiber in the diet, which can eliminate both constipation and diarrhea and detoxify as well as soothe. Psyllium-seed husks are a good choice for sufferers of I.B.S.
• Take a good *acidophilus* tablet daily, which will redress the balance of bacteria in the gut in favor of the beneficial organisms.
• Hydrochloric acid and pepsin, which are often combined, are digestive enzymes that may be taken to alleviate some of the symptoms of I.B.S. Discuss supplementation with your physician before trying this remedy.
• Take a B-complex supplement, which will help you to deal with stress, and also encourage regular control of nerve and muscle function.

• Magnesium relaxes the nerves and also helps to relieve excessive muscle contractions and spasms.
• Antioxidants can help to relieve inflammation and damage to the connective tissue found in the intestinal walls. Vitamin C is healing and mildly anti-inflammatory. Vitamin E is also anti-inflammatory and will help to heal damaged tissue. Selenium works in a complementary way to vitamin E and will help the body to detoxify various harmful compounds.

BELOW *If you suffer from indigestion, avoid eating fatty foods, and do not eat late at night.*

URETHRITIS

Urethritis is an inflammation of the urethra, which is the tube through which urine passes out of the body. Such infection is the most common cause in women, and in men it may also be a symptom of other diseases, including gonnorhea and Reiter's syndrome. Symptoms include a burning sensation and occasionally pain on urinating, blood in the urine and a yellow discharge.

• Fresh garlic, or garlic perles, taken daily, will ease inflammation, and fight infection.
• Drink plenty of water to flush the urinary system.
• Take 1g of vitamin C daily, which acts as a natural diuretic and boosts the immune system. Vitamin C also helps to build healthy mucous membranes.
• Take acidophilus if you have been given a course of antibiotics.

INDIGESTION

Eating too fast, certain foods, and anxiety may all bring on indigestion. Most people suffer from indigestion at some time although pregnant women, heavy smokers, overweight people, and the elderly are particularly prone. Symptoms include abdominal discomfort, a dull ache or stabbing pain in the center of the chest, wind, and heartburn.

• Indigestion is exacerbated by a number of conditions, many of them linked to eating habits.
• Avoid fatty foods, which can make the condition worse, and try to avoid eating late at night, because it means going to bed with a significant amount of undigested food and acid in the stomach.

• Eat a slice of fresh pineapple after meals to ease symptoms. Canned pineapple is not effective.
• Try to ascertain whether or not you have food allergies or intolerances that may be making the problem worse – common culprits are wheat, dairy produce, eggs, citrus fruits, and yeasts.
• Take an *acidophilus* tablet daily to build up the healthy bacteria in the gut, which will insure optimum absorption of nutrients and the health of the gut itself.
• Take a good multivitamin and mineral supplement to insure that all the nutrients required for digestive function are present in adequate quantities.

ABOVE *Eating a slice of fresh pineapple after meals should ease indigestion.*

DIARRHEA

Diarrhea is characterized by frequent, loose stools and is often accompanied by vomiting. The most common cause is an infection of the digestive tract, which leads to gastroenteritis. Gastroenteritis may be caused by eating contaminated food, a viral infection, or be the result of an imbalance in the natural bacterial makeup of the digestive tract.

• Food allergies and intolerance are common causes of diarrhea that is unrelated to illness. If you suspect that you may be intolerant to some foods, see your physician in order to try an exclusion diet. Infections and parasites are other common causes.
• Drink plenty of water, to flush out the system.
• Zinc may reduce gut permeability, if this condition is causing chronic diarrhea to occur.
• Increase your intake of potassium, which is easily lost in diarrhea and

vomiting. Potassium is not usually supplemented, so insure that you get plenty of foods that are rich in the mineral.
• Take extra vitamins B1 and B3 as part of a B-complex supplement, which will address the digestive system.
• Take a good multivitamin and mineral supplement with food when you are able to eat properly again, to replace lost nutrients.
• Take plenty of fresh *acidophilus* for at least a month after an attack, to insure the health of the bowels.

ABOVE *Eat potassium-rich bananas if you have a bout of diarrhea.*

ULCERS

Peptic ulcers are raw spots that develop in the lining of the stomach or duodenum. You are more likely to develop an ulcer if you smoke or drink heavily. A poor diet, stress, and aspirin also contribute to the problem. The main symptom of an ulcer is a gnawing, burning pain in the abdomen.

• It is now believed that a zinc deficiency is a strong causative factor for ulcers, and that vitamin-A supplements may help to protect against chronic gastric ulcers, and reduce the size of any existing ulcers.

• Take plenty of zinc (about 20mg daily), which can accelerate healing.
• Drink plenty of water to help cleanse the digestive system, but avoid drinking with meals, which will dilute the digestive juices and make the process less effective, more time-consuming, and ultimately more painful.

CYSTITIS

Cystitis is an inflammation of the bladder. It is usually caused by a bacterial infection that enters the bladder via the urethra. More women than men suffer from the complaint because the female urethra is shorter and more susceptible to urinary tract infections. Sufferers feel a constant urge to pass water and painful burning sensation on doing so. Other symptoms of cystitis include fever, abdominal pain, a dull backache, and cloudy or blood-stained urine.

• Eat live yogurt, and use a live yogurt douche to ease the symptoms of cystitis and prevent recurrence. By balancing the body's flora it will be more resistant to invading unhealthy bacteria.
• Cranberry juice, drunk daily, will discourage bacteria from sticking to the walls of the bladder and urinary tract. It both treats and prevents the condition. Extract of cranberry tablets are now becoming available.
• Garlic tincture *(see p. 79)* added to food or warm drinks will ease cystitis.
• Drink plenty of water (6 pints/ 3 liters every day) to help flush out the urinary system.
• Take 1g of vitamin C daily, which acts as a natural diuretic and boosts the immune system.

LEFT *Cranberry juice will both prevent and alleviate the symptoms of cystitis.*

Musculoskeletal System

FUELED BY NUTRIENTS AND OXYGEN *from the digestive, respiratory, and circulatory systems, the muscles of the body make movement possible. They are attached to the bones of the skeleton, which they lever around the joints of the body. The bones themselves, as well as the joints between them, are subject to various diseases that can benefit from vitamin and mineral supplements.*

ARTHRITIS

Osteoarthritis is a degenerative disorder that commonly occurs in the weight-bearing joints (the hips, knees, and spine) of older people. The bone cartilage begins to wear away, which causes the underlying bones to become thickened and distorted. At intermittent periods the joint becomes painful, swollen, and stiff, and the condition may become severe enough to interfere with normal life.

• Osteoarthritis becomes more common with age and is usually the result of free-radical damage on the joint cartilage. Taking plenty of antioxidants, such as vitamin C, vitamin E, and beta-carotene, will help to prevent this condition.

• Insure that you get plenty of magnesium and potassium, a deficiency of which can cause muscle weakness and spasms.
• You may also have a vitamin D deficiency, perhaps because of inadequate exposure to the sun, and this should be rectified.
• Zinc and selenium will be required in increased amounts by the body, and should probably be supplemented.

ABOVE *Arthritis sufferers may have vitamin D deficiency. Make sure you have exposure to the sun.*

LEFT *Oily fish, such as mackerel, have been shown to protect against rheumatoid arthritis.*

RHEUMATOID ARTHRITIS

Rheumatoid arthritis is a chronic complaint that affects more women than men. The synovial membrane that surrounds a joint becomes inflamed and swollen, resulting in pain and stiffness in the joint. The small joints in the hand and feet are most commonly affected but rheumatoid arthritis may also be present in other joints such as the wrists, knees, or ankles.

• Magnesium is required to form the synovial fluid that surrounds the joints, and an adequate intake will insure health.
• Large doses of fish oils have been shown to be effective against rheumatoid arthritis, and you will need to insure that you eat plenty of fatty fish as well.
• Supplements of zinc (30mg per day) and selenium (about 250mcg per day) have helped many rheumatoid arthritis sufferers.
• Calcium panthothenate, at 2g every day, may prove useful for some sufferers.
• Copper may help relieve the symptoms of rheumatoid arthritis, and many sufferers use copper bracelets as a result.

RHEUMATISM

Rheumatism is a general term used to describe aches, pains, and stiffness in the bones and muscles. It may be caused by long-term friction, viral infection, stress, food allergies, or environmental factors such as cold and damp.

• Many cases of rheumatism respond to a dietary change, and it suggested that the following foods are eaten as often as possible to reduce muscular and joint inflammation: cabbage, celery, turnip, lemon, dandelion, and oily fish.
• Drink plenty of water, which will flush the system and act as a wonderful detoxificant.

• Avoid members of the "nightshade" family of plants in your diet, since they can cause joint problems. These include paprika, potatoes, peppers, tomatoes, and eggplant.
• Evening primrose oil is a rich source of gamma-linolenic acid, which is necessary for the production of prostaglandins (see p. 82), which may have an anti-inflammatory effect.
• Antioxidants will help to prevent degeneration, which may be causing or exacerbating the condition. Insure that you take a good supplement containing vitamins A, C, and E, as well as the mineral selenium. Zinc may also be useful.

EGGPLANT

POTATOES

ABOVE *Rheumatism sufferers should eliminate members of the nightshade plant family from their diet.*

OSTEOPOROSIS

With osteoporosis the bones waste away and become weak and fragile. The most common cause of osteoporosis is old age, although a sedentary lifestyle, a low-calcium diet, smoking, and too much alcohol may aggravate the condition. More women than men are affected by the disease, primarily because of hormonal changes during the menopause.

• Recent evidence suggests that an increased intake of magnesium may help prevent the worst effects of the bone disease osteoporosis. Magnesium sources include soybeans, nuts, and brewer's yeast.
• Calcium can also be very helpful. Recommended doses are between 1,000 and 1,500mg a day.
• Vitamin D helps the body to absorb calcium.
• Foods containing boron, which reduces the body's excretion of

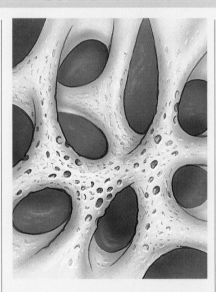

ABOVE *Osteoporosis causes the bones to degenerate, leaving them susceptible to fracture.*

calcium and magnesium, and increases the production of estrogen, should be taken. Try eating pears, prunes, pulses, raisins, tomatoes, and apples, all rich sources.
• Fluoride may be useful for preventing and treating the condition since it stimulates new bone formation. However, insure that you do not take too much (see p. 58), because this can actually encourage the condition.
• Antioxidants will help to control degeneration, so insure that you get an adequate supply of vitamins A, C, and E, and the mineral selenium.
• Research suggests that E.F.A.s are necessary to balance the calcium in our bodies, particularly in the bones. Omega-3 oils may slow down the loss of calcium in the urine, which includes some lost from the bones. Omega-6 oils will help the body to absorb calcium. Try to get the oils from food.

Hormones and Metabolism

HORMONES ARE CHEMICAL *messengers that continuously instruct the body's systems to maintain the status quo. Insulin, for example, is a hormone that helps to keep blood glucose levels stable. Metabolism is the term for the processes within the body that break down and build up substances, releasing and using up energy as they do so to build and fuel the body and its activities.*

GOUT

Uric acid is a waste product of the body and will normally pass out harmlessly through the kidneys. However, if there is an abnormally high level in the system, the excess will form crystals, which are then deposited around the joints. The main symptom of gout is excruciating pain and inflammation of the joint, commonly at the base of the big toe.

• Gout is less common than arthritis, but it can be very painful and debilitating. Insure that you drink plenty of fresh water, during an attack, to help flush toxins from the body, and to encourage the action of the kidneys.
• Vitamin C at 4g daily helps to reduce blood levels of uric acid, and helps to encourage urination.
• Supplements of zinc and magnesium are thought to be useful for gout. Magnesium in particular is responsible for normal hormone activity, which can help to prevent attacks.
• E.F.A.s may be useful for their anti-inflammatory action.
• Charcoal tablets may help to reduce uric acid levels in the body.

CHARCOAL TABLETS

THYROID PROBLEMS

The thyroid gland can be found in the lower neck region. It produces the hormone thyroxine, which controls the rate at which chemical reactions occur in the body. An overactive thyroid (hyperthyroidism) causes these reactions to speed up in the body resulting in irritability, weight loss, heart palpitations, and if untreated, heart failure. Hypo-thyroidism (an underactive thyroid) results in extreme fatigue, weight gain, and general apathy.

• Nutritional deficiencies (for example, zinc, vitamin A, selenium, and iron) and a toxic overload are thought to be the main factors involved in the onset of hypothyroidism. Insure that you eat a good healthy diet, with plenty of fresh organic vegetables, seafood, and onions. Drinking plenty of fresh, filtered water will help the body to flush out toxins.
• Garlic and onions are particularly invaluable when the thyroid gland is underactive.
• Supplement your diet, if advised by your physician, with natural thyroid hormones, and the amino acid tyrosine for hypothyroidism.
• Garlic is rich in iodine, which can help regulate thyroid function.

BELOW *Drink plenty of fresh filtered water to flush toxins from the body.*

HYPOGLYCEMIA

Hypogylcemia is a complaint characterized by an abnormally low level of glucose in the blood (diabetics have the opposite problem – too much glucose in the blood). It usually occurs among insulin-dependent diabetics. Taking too much insulin or not eating correctly can bring on an attack.

• Two common nutritional causes of hypoglycemia are chromium and magnesium deficiency.
• Chromium supplementation at 200mcg per day should raise the blood-sugar level and improve the number of insulin receptors.
• Magnesium will help to improve symptoms and should be taken daily. It is also responsible for normal hormone function and is a common deficiency among pre-menopausal women.

ABOVE *Take brewer's yeast to help regulate blood-sugar levels.*

LEFT *Women of child-bearing age commonly suffer from magnesium deficiency and may need a daily supplement.*

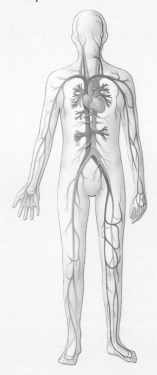

ABOVE *Hypoglycemia occurs when there is too little glucose in the blood.*

DIABETES

Diabetes mellitus is caused by a lack or deficiency of insulin production in the pancreas. As a result the body is unable to process glucose and this causes a high level of glucose in the blood. There are two main forms of diabetes mellitus – insulin-dependent diabetes and insulin-independent diabetes, commonly known as late-onset diabetes.

• Some common nutritional deficiencies associated with diabetes include chromium, vanadium, magnesium, and vitamins C and E. Scientific studies show that high doses of vitamin E improved insulin action in insulin-independent diabetics, and it is believed that high doses of antioxidant nutrients may lead to a regression of late complications of diabetes.
• G.L.A. (gamma-linolenic acid) has been proven to improve symptoms of diabetes significantly.

• Brewer's yeast contains chromium, which helps to normalize blood-sugar levels and metabolism. Take 2 to 3 tablespoons daily.
• Onions and garlic lower blood-sugar levels – insure that you have plenty in your diet; take garlic oil supplements if not.
• High-dose vitamin C supplements (about 1g) have been found to have a beneficial effect on blood-sugar control, and blood lipids (fats).
• Zinc is easily lost in the urine of diabetic people, which may cause poor resistance to infections, poor ability of the body to heal wounds, and in many cases a reduced response to insulin.
• Pyridoxine (vitamin B6) has been used successfully to control diabetes that develops in pregnancy (gestational diabetes).

Mind, Brain, and Nerves

ALL THE MENTAL *and physical activities of the individual are controlled or mediated by the brain and the nervous system. Voluntary actions originate in the brain, and the nerves carry instructions to the muscles, as well as providing the brain with information about our bodies and the world around us. The nervous system relies upon a correct chemical balance within the body, and this can have a significant influence on our mental states as well.*

ANXIETY

Everyone experiences feelings of anxiety at some point in their lives but sometimes these feelings get out of control. This may lead to a whole host of physical and emotional symptoms including high blood pressure, irritability, insomnia, and panic attacks.

• Some of the most common nutritional causes of anxiety and panic attacks include a deficiency of B-complex vitamins, selenium, and magnesium, and sensitivity to sugar and to caffeine.
• Calcium can be very relaxing, and has a role in the transmission of nerve messages. Insure that you have adequate quantities in your diet, and if not, take a supplement of about 400mg per day.
• Increase your intake of B vitamins, which work on the nervous system, and avoid caffeine in any form. B-complex vitamins should be taken at 50mg each.
• Taking 200mg magnesium per day will insure that hormonal activity is normal, and that the chemistry of the nervous system is working efficiently.

SHINGLES

Shingles, or Herpes Zoster, is a viral infection of sensory nerve cells caused by the same virus (varicella-zoster) that causes chicken pox. Shingles occurs most often in people over the age of 50 and may be activated through surgery or X-ray therapy to the spinal cord and its roots. In younger people it is often associated with a weakening of the immune system. Shingles is characterized by pain, which can be disabling, along an affected nerve and its branches and blisters on the skin supplied by the nerve, often occurring around the abdomen, the arm or neck, or sometimes one half of the face.

• Oats, rich in the B-complex vitamins necessary for a healthy nervous system, should be eaten daily. Try to increase your intake of other foods rich in B-complex vitamins.

• Increase your intake of Vitamin C, and take a supplement of 1g up to four times daily.
• Supplementation with Vitamin E is now known to reduce the long-term symptoms associated with shingles – take up to 1,600 iu daily, broken into three doses, with food. Vitamin E oil, applied directly to the sores, will encourage healing.
• An attack of shingles may be a sign of general debility, and you should take steps to boost your immune system to prevent the illness.

RIGHT *Try taking supplements to reduce the incidence of panic attacks in a safe, drug-free way.*

ABOVE *Supplements, such as vitamin E, may help to reduce epileptic seizures in children.*

DEPRESSION

Depression may arise as a result of a traumatic event, such as divorce or bereavement, or it may be caused by everyday worries including financial or relationship problems. Its symptoms include listlessness, insomnia, feelings of intense despair, and lack of confidence. It may also manifest itself in some form of physical illness.

• Depression that occurs just before your menstrual period (P.M.S.) may be caused by a vitamin B6 deficiency; postnatal depression may be caused by a deficiency of vitamin B12, and folic acid.

• Insure you have an adequate intake of vitamin C, which can help to ease the symptoms of depression.

• St. John's wort has been used successfully in the treatment of depression.

• Some therapists may recommend supplementing the amino acid, tryptophan, which is an effective natural relaxant. Eggs, turkey, avocado, bananas, and peanut butter are good sources of tryptophan, and should be considered before supplementation, which is now available only on prescription.

• Chronic depression has been linked to deficiencies of B-complex vitamins, calcium, magnesium, copper, iron, potassium, folic acid, and/or essential fatty acids. Studies show that patients with depression almost always have low levels of one or more of these nutrients. You will probably need to see a nutritionist who will analyze which deficiencies you have, and supplementation will be advised thereafter. In the meantime, a good multivitamin and mineral supplement will help to balance the body.

EPILEPSY

Epilepsy arises from an abnormal function of the brain's communication system. During an epileptic fit, the signals from one group of nerve cells become overwhelmingly strong causing an excessive electrical charge to occur suddenly in the brain. This results in a fit or convulsion, the main symptom of epilepsy. There are two major types of epilepsy – petit mal and grand mal.

• Some common nutritional causes of epilepsy may be allergies, celiac disease, and deficiencies of selenium, magnesium, or vitamins B1, B6, or folic acid.

• Studies show that 400iu vitamin E per day in addition to medication may significantly reduce the number of seizures in epileptic children.

• Many epileptics appear to have low magnesium levels in the blood plasma, and the severity of the epilepsy is directly related to the severity of the deficiency. Extra vitamin B5, magnesium, calcium, and zinc may help to prevent attacks.

• Selenium supplementation was tested in four children in 1991, when anticonvulsant medication was discontinued. Results were good, and the clinical state of the children tested improved in each case.

• Deficiency of vitamins D and B6 can prompt attacks.

• The amino acid taurine has been shown to control seizures.

BELOW *Peanut butter is a good source of tryptophan, which acts as an effective natural relaxant.*

HEADACHES AND MIGRAINE

Headaches are an extremely common complaint and vary in intensity from a mild to severe pain. They can be caused by stress, tiredness, sinusitis, food allergies, eyestrain, physical injury, or too much alcohol. Migraines are severe headaches often accompanied by nausea and disturbed vision. They are often triggered by eating foods that contain tyramine such as bananas, chocolate, cheese, wine, and citrus fruits.

• Frequent headaches could be a signal that you're low on some important vitamins and minerals. Low levels of niacin (vitamin B3) and vitamin B6 can cause headaches, for example, and all the B vitamins are needed to help combat stress and avoid tension headaches. Protein-rich foods such as chicken, fish, beans, peas, milk, cheese, nuts, and peanut butter are all good dietary sources of both niacin and vitamin B6.
• The minerals calcium and magnesium work together to help prevent headaches, especially those related to a woman's menstrual cycle. Good sources of calcium are dairy products, tofu, dark green leafy vegetables such as kale or broccoli, and beans and peas. Magnesium is found in dark green leafy vegetables, nuts, bananas, wheatgerm, seafood, and beans and peas. If you can't eat some of these foods because they are headache triggers, taking a good daily multivitamin with minerals should provide enough of all the nutrients you need to prevent headaches.
• The herbs ginger and feverfew are both excellent preventive measures and remedies for migraine. Fresh ginger, which can be chewed during an attack, helps to dilate blood vessels that have constricted. Feverfew, taken daily, can reduce the incidence and severity of attacks. If you take feverfew fresh, eat the leaf between slices of bread because fresh feverfew can be hard on the stomach.

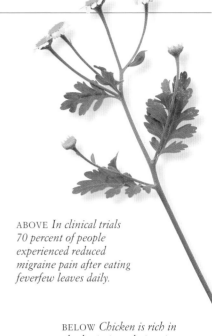

ABOVE *In clinical trials 70 percent of people experienced reduced migraine pain after eating feverfew leaves daily.*

BELOW *Chicken is rich in both niacin and vitamin B6. Include it in your diet if you think you may be lacking in either of these.*

HYPERACTIVITY

Hyperactivity is much more common in children than in adults. The hyperactive child is excessively energetic and sleeps very little. He or she will also find it difficult to concentrate for very long and is easily distracted. Behavior may be impulsive and aggressive, and tantrums are extremely common.

• Some of the most common nutritional causes of hyperactivity include candidiasis, chemical sensitivities, deficiencies of zinc, B-vitamins, magnesium, chromium, and E.F.A.s, food intolerances or allergies, and a sensitivity to sugar.
• It will be necessary to see a nutritional therapist who can ascertain which deficiencies are most common and prescribe supplements, or alter the diet accordingly. Because hyperactivity most often affects children, it is important that the diet is monitored carefully, and any exclusions overseen by a registered therapist. There have been many promising studies, however, with supplementation of E.F.A.s, and with diets that excluded common allergens and food additives, many of which lower levels both of E.F.A.s and of zinc in the body.

STROKE

A stroke occurs when the blood supply to the brain becomes disturbed either through thrombosis, embolism, or hemorrhage. The brain may be permanently damaged and result in loss of speech or movement. Damage is usually restricted to one side of the body. This is because only one side of the brain is damaged; the right side of the brain controls the left side of the body and vice versa.

• It is now believed that a flavonoid deficiency may be at the root of a stroke, and evidence now shows that vitamin E can reduce the stickiness of the platelets by more than 80 percent.
• It is recommended that you take vitamin C with bioflavonoids, at 1g per day, which can help prevent stroke and encourage recovery if you do have one.
• Vitamin E at 400iu per day is believed to be adequate to prevent stroke in susceptible individuals.
• Fish oils, magnesium, and B-complex vitamins may also help to prevent the condition.
• Refer also to heart disease, (see p.123).

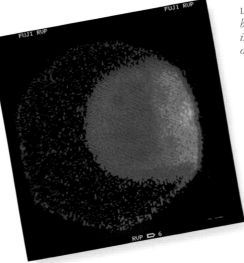

LEFT *During a stroke, the blood supply to the brain is interrupted, causing loss of speech or movement.*

RIGHT *If you are unable to sleep, try eating lots of raw vegetables to cleanse the system.*

INSOMNIA

Insomnia, or inability to get to sleep, affects everyone at some time. It is usually related to anxiety or stress. Continual lack of sleep will lead to many other problems, such as inability to concentrate, chronic tiredness, and depression.

• Some of the nutritional causes of insomnia include a B-vitamin deficiency, a magnesium deficiency, and a toxic overload. Insure that you drink plenty of water to help your body to flush out toxins, and eat plenty of fresh fruits and vegetables, preferably raw, which are very cleansing. Garlic is too, and may help if you do have too many toxins in your body.

• Increase your intake of vitamins B, C, and folic acid, and of the mineral zinc. Make sure you have a good intake of all vitamins and minerals, to insure that your fatigue isn't caused by deficiency.
• Magnesium should be taken at 200mg daily, and zinc at 15mg daily.
• B12 should be taken as part of a good B-complex supplement to insure normal sleeping patterns.
• Calcium should be increased, and some experts suggest a calcium supplement just before bedtime.
• Tryptophan, an amino acid, helps to encourage healthy sleep – good sources include avocado, turkey, bananas, or peanut butter.

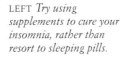

LEFT *Try using supplements to cure your insomnia, rather than resort to sleeping pills.*

Reproductive System: Female

THE FEMALE REPRODUCTIVE ORGANS *are designed for conception, pregnancy, and childbirth. Our bodies secrete varying amounts of different hormones in a distinct, monthly cycle. If fertilization and pregnancy have not occurred, hormone levels decrease, the uterine lining is shed, and the cycle begins anew. Ovarian hormone release is regulated by the pituitary gland in the brain, so stress can affect the menstrual cycle.*

RIGHT *Both parents should follow a healthy diet to insure that sperm and ova are healthy.*

INFERTILITY

Infertility or inability to conceive is a problem for many women. The most common cause of infertility in women is failure to ovulate (release an egg). This is usually due to hormonal problems. Other common causes include damaged ovaries or Fallopian tubes or structural problems with the uterus such as fibroids or endometriosis.

• Eating plenty of wholefoods, rich in vitamins and minerals, will insure not only that sperm and egg are healthy but also that the woman's body is a welcoming home for the growing embryo. Good nutrition increases the chances of conception and gives the baby every chance of being healthy.
• Vitamin E may regulate the production of cervical mucus.
• An increased intake of E.F.A.s (essential fatty acids, found in oily fish, fish-liver oils, seeds, nuts, pulses, beans, evening primrose oil, and unrefined vegetable oils) can stimulate the production of sex hormones.
• Women should supplement 500mg of vitamin C, twice daily, and 15mg of zinc.

MENSTRUAL PROBLEMS

Common period problems include dysmenorrhea (painful periods), menorrhagia (excessive menstrual flow), and amenorrhea (scanty or absent periods). Dysmenorrhea is characterized by cramps in the abdominal region that are caused by uterine contractions. Heavy menstrual bleeding is also commonly associated with cramping pains and may be so severe as to interfere with normal life. Amenorrhea is very common during both the early pubescent years and the menopause but may also be caused by weight loss, stress, nutritional deficiency, or hormonal imbalance.

• Vitamin B6, taken twice daily, can help prevent period pains. Take one 50mg B-complex tablet daily.
• Magnesium will help with period pains and should be taken at 200mg per day.

• Evening primrose oil and fish oils, both at 500mg per day, can reduce period problems, including heavy periods and pain and cramping.
• Agnus castus will help to balance the hormones. Take 25 drops of the tincture three times daily with food.
• Iron (5mg daily – more if you tend to lose a lot of blood) and zinc (15mg) will help in cases of heavy menstrual periods.
• Take vitamin A (about 5,000iu should be sufficient) and B6 for heavy menstrual periods.
• Bioflavonoids can help to balance hormone levels and regulate the menstrual cycle. Take as part of a good vitamin C with bioflavonoids supplement, or increase your intake of bioflavonoid-rich foods (*see p. 85*).
• Deficiencies of zinc and vitamin B6 can often result in absence of periods.

PREGNANCY-RELATED PROBLEMS

Many women experience a variety of problems during pregnancy. These discomforts are largely the result of hormonal changes in the body or because the body is under additional strain during pregnancy. Common complaints include anemia, constipation, cramps, varicose veins, vaginal thrush, stretchmarks, and nausea and vomiting.

• Insure that you get plenty of iron (see your physician for dosages), to prevent and treat anemia. Take vitamin C (500mg per day) with iron to aid absorption.
• Folic acid (at least 400mcg per day) is necessary during pregnancy for the healthy development of the fetus.
• An increase in dietary fiber will help to prevent constipation.
• Eat plenty of foods rich in calcium to prevent cramp.
• E.F.A.s are vital for growth and development of the baby, particularly for the brain and nervous system. Adequate intakes of E.F.A.s in the newborn appear to influence vision and intelligence.

• Vitamin A is linked to growth, and it is now recommended that all pregnant and lactating mothers take supplements of vitamin A as beta-carotene (no more than 10,000iu per day), as well as vitamins D and C, in order to build up vitamin stores that can be passed across the placenta.
• Zinc deficiency during pregnancy is related to low birthweight babies, and it is recommended that you take 15mg per day.
• Vitamins C and E and bioflavonoids, zinc, and brewer's yeast will help to heal damaged blood vessels causing varicose veins.
• Take *acidophilus* for thrush, or eat plenty of live yogurt, and also apply live yogurt to the affected area.
• Insure you have plenty of vitamins E, C, zinc, silica, and panthothenic acid, which can help to prevent stretchmarks. Vitamin E oil can be applied neat to areas that are likely to become stretched, including the abdomen and perineum.
• Nausea and vomiting in pregnancy will usually respond to 10mg zinc daily, 5mg iron, 100mg magnesium, and 200mcg folic acid.

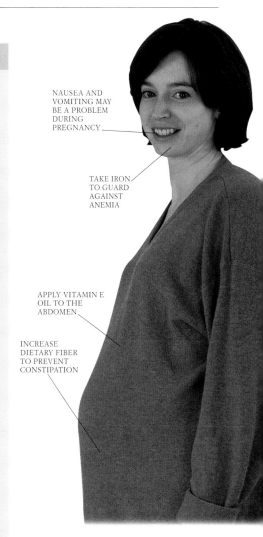

NAUSEA AND VOMITING MAY BE A PROBLEM DURING PREGNANCY

TAKE IRON TO GUARD AGAINST ANEMIA

APPLY VITAMIN E OIL TO THE ABDOMEN

INCREASE DIETARY FIBER TO PREVENT CONSTIPATION

ABOVE *Most women experience at least some niggling discomforts during pregnancy.*

PREMENSTRUAL SYNDROME

Premenstrual syndrome relates to a whole host of physical and emotional symptoms that occur between ovulation and menstruation. Physical symptoms include fluid retention, tender breasts, poor skin, and headaches. Women may also become weepy, depressed, and even suicidal in extreme circumstances. P.M.S is believed to be primarily caused by a hormonal imbalance in the body.

• Evening primrose oil has been very effective in alleviating premenstrual breast tenderness, edema, and eczema. Take six to eight 500mg capsules per day, for at least four months.
• Vitamin B-complex will help with nervous tension, and should be taken at 50 to 100mg per day.

EVENING PRIMROSE OIL CAPSULES

• Linseed oil will help with dry and rough skin: take 1 tablespoon a day.
• Magnesium, taken twice a day at 500mg, will help with insomnia, palpitations, and period pains.
• Zinc should be taken at 15mg daily throughout your cycle.
• Agnus castus will help to balance hormones. Take 25 drops of the tincture three times daily with food.
• Chromium may help with symptoms related to blood sugar.

MENOPAUSE PROBLEMS

The menopause marks the end of a woman's reproductive years and may be accompanied by many uncomfortable emotional and physical symptoms. These include hot flushes, headaches, heavy periods, irritability and mood swings, and pain during intercourse, mostly as a result of vaginal dryness. Hormonal changes (a decrease in estrogen and progesterone) in the body are the cause of most of these complaints.

• Linseed oil, evening primrose, vitamin B-complex (50mg daily), and zinc (15mg daily) can be taken for skin problems.
• Magnesium is helpful for insomnia and sleep problems – take 200mg daily.

• Agnus castus herb (about 25 drops of tincture, three times daily) will balance the hormones and help to relieve the symptoms of the menopause.
• Take magnesium and vitamin B-complex for anxiety and irritability.
• Vitamin E, linseed oil, *acidophilus*, and vitamin B-complex will help with tender and lumpy breasts.
• Vitamin C (500 to 1,000mg per day) can be useful for constipation.
• Coenzyme Q10 will be useful for lack of energy and fatigue; check that you are not anemic.
• Quercetin can help with migraine and headaches associated with menopause, as can vitamin C and E.

• Vitamin C can help regulate heavy bleeding (flooding), when combined with bioflavonoids. Vitamin A (about 1,000iu), zinc, iron, and vitamin B-complex can also help with heavy menstrual periods.
• Selenium, as part of a good antioxidant supplement, may help to reduce hot flushes and night sweats, as will vitamin C which is more effective than H.R.T. in preventing these symptoms.
• Zinc, vitamin C, (500g per day), vitamin E (200iu per day), and magnesium will help with painful menstrual periods.
• A vitamin E capsule can be placed inside the vagina, as required, for vaginal dryness.

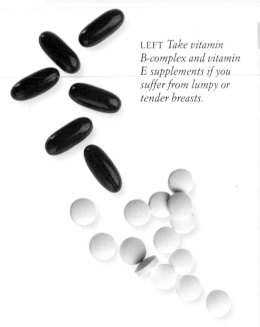

LEFT *Take vitamin B-complex and vitamin E supplements if you suffer from lumpy or tender breasts.*

VAGINAL THRUSH

The symptoms of vaginal thrush include a dry, red, itchy vulva and a white discharge. The complaint is caused by the yeast-like organism *Candida albicans*, which occurs naturally in warm and moist parts of the body and poses a problem only when it becomes too proliferate. Thrush commonly occurs after a course of antibiotics since these drugs kill the intestinal flora that keep candida under control.

• Take echinacea three times daily for chronic cases of thrush, and every two hours in acute attacks, to boost the immune system.

• Take *acidophilus* tablets to restore the healthy bacteria in the body, which will fight the infection.
• A live yogurt douche will encourage the growth of healthy bacteria (flora), which will prevent fungal infection. Use regularly if you are prone to thrush.
• Consider a yeast-free multivitamin and mineral supplement if you have recurrent thrush.
• A supplement of zinc, at 20mg per day, can help, as can a supplement of iron, such as ferrous sulfate, 200mg once or twice a day, especially if heavy periods have been a problem.

RIGHT *You could use a live yogurt douche if you experience recurrent bouts of vaginal thrush.*

Reproductive System: Male

THE MALE REPRODUCTIVE ORGANS *lie partially inside the lower abdomen (prostate, vas deferens), and partially outside (penis and scrotum, which contains the testes). The testes produce sperm, which are needed to fertilize the eggs of the female. In men, the reproductive organs are closely connected with the urinary system, and the urethra transports both seminal fluid and urine.*

INFERTILITY

Male infertility accounts for approximately 30 percent of the problems encountered by couples who are unable to conceive.

• Studies in the United States have shown that zinc is essential for sperm formation, and men who have zinc deficiencies may produce zero or reduced sperm counts. Zinc is also linked to the male sex drive, and most men are advised to take supplemental zinc when trying to achieve a pregnancy.
• Eating plenty of wholefoods, rich in vitamins and minerals, will insure that the sperm are healthy.
• Vitamins E and B6 may be supplemented, which are often linked to a low sperm count.
• An increased intake of E.F.A.s (found in oily fish, fish-liver oils, seeds, nuts, pulses, beans, evening primrose oil, and unrefined vegetable oils) can stimulate the production of sex hormones.
• Men suffering from infertility should take a selenium supplement, which can improve sperm mobility.
• Men with a low vitamin C intake have an increased likelihood of genetic damage to their sperm.
• Men should take 500mg of vitamin C, twice daily, and also 15mg of zinc.

RIGHT *Include zinc-rich foods, such as oysters, in your diet to guard against prostate problems.*

PROSTATE ENLARGEMENT AND PROSTATITIS

The prostate is a small sex gland that surrounds the urethra at the point where it leaves the bladder. Benign prostatic hypertophy, or enlarged prostate, is a noncancerous growth that causes the flow of urine to become obstructed. Prostatitis, inflammation of the prostate gland, commonly occurs after an urinary-tract infection has spread to the prostate. Its symptoms include a frequent urge to urinate, difficulty in urinating, and a pain around the base of the penis.

• Some of the most common nutritional causes of prostate conditions include a deficiency of essential fatty acids, a toxic overload, and a zinc deficiency.

• Pollen extract is believed to have anti-inflammatory and hormonal properties, and in one study has successfully provided relief from chronic prostatitis in 15 patients.
• A decrease in zinc levels has been implicated in prostate abnormalities. It is recommended that you take zinc at 15mg per day, and take selenium as part of a good antioxidant supplement to reduce cadmium levels, which studies show to be high in many cases of prostate abnormality.
• Take 500mg fish oil and 500mg evening primrose oil per day for prostate enlargement, along with saw palmetto, a herb that has been used traditionally against prostate enlargement. Studies show that it inhibits the processes that encourage prostate enlargement.

Further Reading

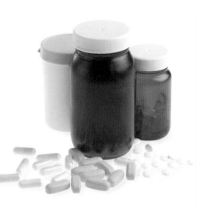

ADAMS, RUTH,
*The Complete Home Guide
to All the Vitamins,*
Larchmont Books, 1972

BALCH, JAMES F., M.D.,
and PHYLLIS A.,
*Prescription for Nutritional
Healing,*
Avery Publishing Group
Inc., 1990

BRUNING, NANCY
PAULINE,
*The Natural Health Guide to
Antioxidants: Using
Vitamins and Other
Supplements to Fight
Disease, Boost Immunity,
and Maintain Optimal
Health,*
Bantam Books, 1994

BRYCE-SMITH, DEREK
and LIZ HODGKINSON,
The Zinc Solution,
Arrow Books, 1987

CARPER, JEAN, FOOD:
Your Miracle Medicine,
Simon & Schuster, 1993

DAVIS, STEPHEN
and ALAN STEWART,
Nutritional Medicine,
Pan Books, 1987

EBON, MARTIN,
*Which Vitamins
Do You Need?,*
Bantam Books, 1974

ERDMANN, ROBERT
and MEIRION JONES,
The Amino Revolution,
Century, 1987

FEINSTEIN, ALICE (ED.),
*Prevention's Healing with
Vitamins: The Most Effective
Vitamin and Mineral
Treatments for Everyday
Health Problems and
Serious Disease,*
Rodale Press, 1998

HENDLER, SHELDON
SAUL, M.D., PH.D,
*The Physicians' Vitamin
and Mineral Encyclopedia,*
Simon & Schuster, 1995

KENTON, LESLIE and
SUSANNAH,
Raw Energy,
Arrow Books, 1991

LAZARIDES, LINDA,
The Nutritional Health Bible,
Thorsons, 1997

LIEBERMAN, SHARI, and
BRUNING, NANCY
PAULINE,
*The Real Vitamin and
Mineral Book: Using
Supplements for Optimum
Health,*
Avery, 1997

LOWE, CARL,
The Complete Vitamin Book,
Berkley, 1994

MATTHEWS, KATHY, and
GILLER, ROBERT M.,
*Natural Prescriptions: Dr
Giller's Natural Treatments
and Vitamin Therapies for
More than 100 Common
Ailments,*
Ballantine Books, 1995

MERVYN, LEONARD,
*Thorson's Complete Guide to
Vitamins and Minerals,*
Thorsons, 1995

MINDELL, EARL,
The Vitamin Bible,
Arrow, 1993

MORSE, ELIZABETH,
JOHN RIVERS, AND
ANNE HEUGHAN,
Food and Health,
Barrie & Jenkins, 1990

MORTIMORE, DENISE,
*In a Nutshell:
Nutritional Healing,*
Element Books, 1998

MORTIMORE, DENISE,
*The Complete
Illustrated Guide to
Nutritional Healing,*
Element Books, 1998

RODALE, J. I.,
*The Complete Book of
Minerals for Health,*
Rodale Books, 1976

ROSENBAUM,
DR. MICHAEL E. and
BOSCO, DOMINIC,
*The Super
Supplements Bible,*
Thorsons, 1998

ROSENBERG, HAROLD
and A. N. FELDZAMAN,
*Physician's Book of
Vitamin Therapy:
Megavitamins for Health,*
Putnam's, 1974

SHAW, NON
*Herbalism:
An Illustrated Guide,*
Element Books, 1998

STEWART, MARYON
and DR. ALAN, EVERY
*Woman's Health Guide –
The Women's Nutritional
Advisory Service Handbook
for Drug-free Health,*
Headline, 1995

VAN STRATEN, MICHAEL
and BARBARA GRIGGS,
Superfoods,
Dorling Kindersley, 1992

WALJI, HASNAIN,
*The Vitamin Guide:
Using Vitamins for
Optimum Health,*
Element Books, 1992

Useful Addresses

AUSTRALASIA

**Australian College
of Nutritional and
Environmental Medicine**
13 Hilton Street
Beaumaris
Victoria 3193
Australia
Tel: 9589 6088

**Australian Natural
Therapists Association**
Taren Point
PO Box 2517
Sydney 2232
Australia

**Association of Natural
Therapies**
82 Forrest Hill Road
Milford
Auckland
New Zealand

Society of Naturopaths
Box 19183
Auckland 7
New Zealand

EUROPE

**British Association of
Nutritional Therapists**
c/o SPNT
PO Box 47
Heathfield
East Sussex TN21 8ZX
U. K.
Send £2 for a register of
practitioners

**British Society for Allergy,
Environmental and Nutri-
tional Medicine**
PO Box 28
Totton
Southampton
Hants S040 2ZA
U. K.

**Society for the Promotion
of Nutritional Therapy**

PO Box 47
Heathfield
East Sussex TN21 8ZX
Tel: 01825 872971
U. K.
E-mail and Internet:
100045.255@Compuserve.
com

Educational and
campaigning organization
with branches throughout
the U.K. and members in
many foreign countries.
Publishes quarterly journal
Nutritional Therapy Today
for members. Factsheets and
other publications also
available. Send £15
(U.K./Europe) and £24 (rest
of the world) to join the
society for one year.

**National Institute
of Medical Herbalists**
56 Longbrook Street
Exeter
Devon EX4 6AH
.U. K.
Tel: 01392 426022
Send large S. S.A.E. and two
stamps for a register of
practitioners

NORTH AMERICA

**American Academy
of Environmental Medicine**
4510 West 89th Street
Prairie Village,
Kansas 66207
U.S.A.
Tel: 913 341 3625
Register of practitioners of
environmental medicine.

**American College of
Advancement in Medicine**
PO Box 3427
Laguna Hills
CA 92654
U.S.A.
Tel: 174 583 7666

**American
Dietetic Association**
216 W. Jackson Blvd.
Suite 800
Chicago
IL 60606
U.S.A.
Tel: 312 899 0040

**American Preventive
Medical Association**
275 Millway
PO Box 732
Banstable
Maine 02630
U.S.A.
Tel: 508 362 4343

HealthComm International
PO Box 1729
Gig Harbor
Washington 98335
U.S.A.
Tel: 206 851 3943

**International Society for
Orthomolecular Medicine**
16 Florence Avenue
Toronto, Ontario
M2N 1E9
Canada
Tel: 416 733 2117

**National Institute of
Nutrition**
Suite 400
2565 Carling Avenue
Ottawa, Ontario
Canada
K1Z 8RI
Tel: 613 235 3355

Index

A

acidophilus 76
  A.I.D.S. 120
  anemia 122
  cancer 93
  cold sores 117
  digestive system 124, 125, 126, 127
  elderly people 105
  fatigue 121
  menopause 138
  pregnancy 137
  vaginal thrush 138
  weight loss 97
acne 30, 52, 64, 76, 116
acne rosacea 32
aging 104–5
  antioxidants 19, 94–5
  coenzyme Q10 73
  evening primrose oil 83
  pollen 74
  vitamins 30, 38, 40
  zinc 52
agnus castus 111, 136, 137, 138
A.I.D.S. 64, 120
alcohol 32, 33, 34, 93, 95, 99, 101
alcoholism 52, 67, 71, 83
algae 72, 101, 121
allergies 11, 25, 120
  asthma 118
  bee products 74, 75
  digestive system 125, 126, 127
  echinacea 78
  flavonoids 85
  gingko 80
  minerals 46, 52
  skin problems 117
  vitamins 34, 38
alpha tocopherol *see* vitamin E
Alzheimer's disease 45, 61, 73
amino acids 23, 28, 66–71, 74
anemia 122
  minerals 48, 52, 56, 61, 62
  vitamin B 32, 34, 35, 36, 37, 55
anorexia 52
antioxidants 16, 18–19, 85
  aging 94, 105, 129
  asthma 118
  bowel problems 125
  cancer 93
  prostrate problems 139
  rheumatism 129
  skin problems 116
  when to take 21
  women 111
anxiety 45, 50, 56, 71, 132, 138

appetite problems 37, 63, 69, 74, 81, 97
L-arginine 66
arthritis 128
  amino acids 68
  E.F.A.s 82
  minerals 52, 54, 56, 61, 64
  vitamins 34, 40
ascorbic acid *see* vitamin C
L-aspartic acid 67
asthma 118
  E.F.A.s 82
  Gingko biloba 80
  minerals 50, 64
  vitamins 33, 35, 38
astragalus 89
atherosclerosis 61, 79

B

babies 16, 108–9
bacteria, live 76–7, 120
bee products 74–5, 97, 101, 121, 139
beta-carotene 30, 94, 111, 128, 137
bifidus 77
bioflavonoids *see* flavonoids
biotin 44
blood clots 38, 43, 82, 123
blood pressure, high 33, 46, 50, 60, 79, 122
bone disease 42, 46, 129
  see also osteoporosis
boron 54, 111, 129
bowel problems 74, 76, 79, 84, 95, 125
breast problems 40, 59, 82, 138
breathing problems 118–19
bronchitis 118
bruising 85
burns 38, 40, 66

C

caffeine 31, 32, 34, 91, 95, 101, 132
calciferol *see* vitamin D
calcium 46–7, 93, 103
  anxiety 132
  cancer 93
  headaches 134
  high blood pressure 122
  insomnia 103, 135
  men 113
  osteoporosis 129
  pregnancy 137
  rheumatoid arthritis 128
  when to take 21
  women 111
cancer 91–2
  E.F.A.s 82
  fiber 84

garlic 79
  minerals 52, 56, 64
  vitamins 38, 40
carbohydrates 13, 14
L-carnitine 68
carpal tunnel syndrome 32, 35
cataracts 19, 32, 70
chelated products 23
children 108–9, 115, 133, 134
cholesterol 15
  bee products 75
  bifidus 77
  fiber 84
  ginseng 81
  heart disease 123
  minerals 50, 56
  vitamins 33, 38, 45
choline 45, 99
chromium 56
  heart disease 123
  hypoglycemia 131
  men 113
  premenstrual syndrome 137
  weight loss 97
  women 111
circulatory problems 33, 79, 80, 82, 85, 122–3
cirrhosis 45
cobalamin *see* vitamin B12
cobalt 55
coenzyme Q10 19, 73
  cancer 93
  energy 91
  heart disease 123
  high blood pressure 122
  immune system 120
  menopause 138
  weight loss 97
coenzyme R *see* biotin
cold sores 117
colds and flu 119
  flavonoids 85
  propolis 75
  vitamins 30, 38, 42
  zinc 52
confusion 37, 63
conjunctivitis 42
contraceptive pill 110
convalescence 34, 36, 37
copper 57, 111, 113, 122, 128
crohn's disease 124
L-cysteine 67
cystitis 127

D

deficiencies 16–17, 25, 27
dementia 37
depression 133
  amino acids 67, 69, 70, 71
  E.F.A.s 83

gingko biloba 80
  minerals 50, 56, 65
  St. John's wort 133
  vitamins 33, 36, 38, 45
dermatitis 44
detoxification 18–19, 66, 81, 103, 130
diabetes 131
  coenzyme Q10 73
  fiber 84
  minerals 50, 56, 61, 65
  vitamins 31, 33, 38, 40, 44, 45
diarrhea 127
diet
  healthy 12–13, 93, 114
  special 15
  Western 9, 11, 15
dieticians 25
digestive system 36, 124–7
dosage 20, 21, 29, 115

E

E.A.R. (estimated average requirement) 29
echinacea 78, 89, 119, 120, 121, 138
eczema 44, 45, 83, 117
elderly people 104–5
energy 90–1
  bee products 74, 75
  coenzyme Q10 73
  ginseng 81
  minerals 50, 56
epilepsy 31, 40, 61, 64, 133
essential fatty acids (E.F.A.) 82–3
  blood pressure 122
  cancer 93
  chronic fatigue 121
  eczema 117
  fertility 136, 139
  gout 130
  heart disease 123
  hyperactivity 134
  osteoporosis 129
  pregnancy 137
  Raynaud's disease 123
evening primrose oil 83
  eczema 117
  elderly people 105
  menopause 138
  menstrual problems 136
  premenstrual syndrome 111, 137
  prostrate problems 139
  rheumatism 129
eyes 19, 30, 32, 42, 50, 70

F

fat-soluble vitamins 14, 30
fatigue 37, 48, 50, 67, 90–1, 121

fats 13, 14, 15, 93, 95
fertility 69
    female 41, 136
    male 52, 64, 66, 75, 107,
        113, 139
fiber 15, 84
    aging 95
    bowel problems 125, 137
    cancer 93
    heart disease 123
    weight loss 97
fish oils 82
    blood pressure 122
    elderly people 105
    fatigue 121
    menstrual problems 136
    prostrate problems 139
    psoriasis 116
    Raynaud's disease 123
    rheumatoid arthritis 128
    stroke 135
flavonoids 19, 80, 85, 135,
    136, 137, 138
fluid retention 35, 83
fluorine 58, 129
folic acid 36, 107, 122, 133, 137
food, nutritional value 12–15
food intolerances 11, 25
    asthma 118
    digestive system 125, 126,
        127
    indigestion 126
    skin problems 116, 117
food poisoning 36, 127
free radicals 18–19, 28, 92
fruit 13, 15, 19
fungal infections 54, 75, 76

G
garlic 79
    aging 94, 105
    bowel problems 125
    cancer 93
    cold sores 117
    colds and flu 119
    cystitis 127
    detoxification 135
    diabetes 131
    heart disease 111, 113,
        123
    high blood pressure 122
    immune system 89, 121
    thyroid problems 130
ginger 91, 97, 123, 134
ginkgo biloba 19, 80
    allergies 120
    asthma 118
    memory/aging 91, 94, 99
ginseng 81
    energy 91, 94, 111
    heart disease 123
    immune system 89, 121
    memory 99
    stress 101, 111
glandular fever 121
L-glutamine 67
glycine 68
goiter 59, 72
gotu kola 91, 99
gout 130

growth problems 48, 52
gum problems 10, 50, 73

H
hair problems 44, 45, 64
hands, numbness 35, 123
headaches 33, 134, 138
hearing 48, 50, 52, 80, 94
heart disease 123
    coenzyme Q10 73
    fiber 84
    garlic 79
    men 112, 113
    minerals 46, 56, 61
    vitamins 35, 40
hemorrhoids 125
hepatitis 64
herbalism 26
herbs 78, 81, 101, 103, 134
herpes 52, 66, 69
    cold sores 117
    glandular fever 121
    shingles 31, 40
L-histidine 68
H.I.V. 120
hormones 130–1
hyperactivity 134
hypoglycemia 46, 50, 56, 68,
    131

I
immune system 10, 88–9,
    120–1
    amino acids 66, 68
    bee products 74, 75
    coenzyme Q10 73
    echinacea 78
    E.F.A.s 82
    garlic 79
    minerals 40, 48, 52
    vitamins 30, 34, 36, 38, 40
indigestion 126
infertility see fertility
inositol 45
insomnia 46, 50, 71, 81,
    102–3, 135
iodine 59, 72, 111, 113, 130
iron 48–9
    anemia 122
    crohn's disease 124
    energy 91
    menstrual problems 111,
        136
    pregnancy 137
    vaginal thrush 138
    when to take 21
irritability 37, 63, 83, 138
irritable bowel syndrome
    125

K
kidney problems 35, 50, 64,
    82

L
lecithin 99
legs 35, 48, 70

linoleic acid 82
linolenic acid 82, 129, 131
liver problems 45, 66, 81, 83
L-lysine 69, 121

M
magnesium 47, 50–1
    A.I.D.S. 120
    allergies 120
    anxiety 132
    arthritis 128
    asthma 118
    bowel problems 125
    diabetes 131
    energy levels 91
    epilepsy 133
    gout 130
    headaches 134
    heart disease 123
    high blood pressure 122
    hypoglycemia 131
    immune system 121
    insomnia 103, 135
    memory 99
    men 113
    menopause 138
    menstrual problems 136
    osteoporosis 129
    pregnancy 137
    premenstrual syndrome
        137
    Raynaud's disease 123
    stroke 135
    when to take 21
    women 111
manganese 61, 111, 113
M.E. 75, 121
megadosing 20
memory 45, 80, 81, 98–9
men 112–13
    fertility 52, 64, 66, 75,
        107, 113, 139
Ménière's syndrome 33
menopause 41, 54, 83, 111,
    138
menstrual problems 136
    flavonoids 85
    minerals 46, 48, 50
    vitamins 33, 40, 43
mental problems 33, 35, 61,
    132–3
metabolism 130–1
L-methionine 69
migraine 33, 42, 46, 50, 70,
    134
minerals 8, 28, 46–65
molybdenum 62, 111, 113
mononucleosis 121
multiple sclerosis 37, 68, 83
multivitamins, when to take
    21
muscles
    building 54, 66, 69
    cramps 35, 46, 70
    myasthenia gravis 61
    pain 44, 50
    spasms 35
muscular dystrophy 40, 64,
    68, 75

musculoskeletal system 128–9
myalgic encephalomyelitis
    75, 121

N
naturopathy 8–9
nervous system 132–3
    amino acids 69
    coenzyme Q10 73
    ginseng 81
    minerals 55, 60
    vitamins 31, 35
neuralgia 31, 40, 70
niacin see vitamin B3
nutritional therapists 11, 17,
    24–5, 86–71, 115, 141
nutritional therapy 8–9,
    10–11, 114–15

O
oats 91
obesity 73, 83, 84, 96–7
omega oils 82, 116, 129
organic produce 13, 15
osteoarthritis 40, 128
osteoporosis 46, 50, 54, 58,
    63, 111, 129

P
pain
    amino acids 70
    growing 46
    muscles 44, 50
    post-operative 31
    propolis 75
    vitamins 36, 37
panic attacks 71, 132
panthothenic acid see
    vitamin B5
Parkinson's disease 35, 40
Dl-phenylalanine 70
L-phenylalanine 69, 97
phosphorus 47, 63
phylloquinone 43
piles 125
P.M.S. see premenstrual
    syndrome
pollen 74, 97, 101, 121, 139
pollution 11, 40, 42, 107, 118
polyphenols 85
post-operative shock 34
potassium 60, 122, 127, 128
pregnancy 106–7, 137
    iron 48
    morning sickness 35
    vitamins 30, 36, 41
premenstrual syndrome 137
    amino acids 71
    evening primrose 83, 111
    minerals 50, 56, 111
    vitamins 35, 40, 111, 133
proanthocyanidins 19
probiotics 76
propolis 75
prostate 50, 74, 113, 139
protein 13, 14
psoriasis 30, 42, 82, 83, 116
pyridoxine 35, 131

Q

quercetin 19, 138

R

Raynaud's disease 123
R.D.A. (recommended
    dietary allowance) 27, 29
R.D.I. (reference nutrient
    intake) 27, 29
reproductive system
    female 136–8
    male 139
retinol 30
rheumatism 56, 129
rheumatoid arthritis 34, 83,
    128
riboflavin see vitamin B2
royal jelly 75, 89, 91, 121

S

safety 29, 87, 115
saw palmetto 139
schizophrenia 33, 61, 66, 68
seaweed 72
selenium 64
    acne 116
    aging 94
    A.I.D.S. 120
    anxiety 132
    arthritis/rheumatism 128,
        129
    digestive system 124, 125
    epilepsy 133
    fertility 139
    glandular fever 121
    immune system 89
    men 113
    menopause 138
    prostrate problems 139
    women 111
self-help 114–15
sexual problems 62, 69, 75,
    80, 81
shingles 31, 40
skin problems 116–17
    E.F.A.s 82, 83
    pollen 74
    vitamins 30, 32, 33, 35, 36
sleep 46, 50, 71, 81, 102–3,
    135
smoking 26, 40, 67, 93, 95,
    99, 101, 118
stress 95, 100–1
    ginseng 81
    L-tyrosine 71
    minerals 47, 50
    vitamins 32, 34, 38
stroke 135
supplements
    dosage 21, 26–7, 29
    types 11, 22–3
    using 12–13, 86–7,
        114–15
    when to take 20–1

T

taurine 70, 133
teeth 42, 47, 50, 58, 73
thiamine see vitamin B1
thyroid function 52, 59, 64,
    130
time-release supplements 20,
    21, 23
tinnitus 33, 37, 52, 80
Tired All the Time (T.A.T.)
    syndrome 34, 90
toxins 11
    ginseng 81
    insomnia 103, 135
    memory 99
    overload 18, 25
    pregnancy 107
    vitamin c 38
L-tryptophan 71, 103, 133, 135
L-tyrosine 71, 101, 130

U

ubiquinone see coenzyme
    Q10
ulcers
    gastric 30, 127
    mouth 33, 36, 52
    peptic 67, 127
urinary system 127

V

vaginal problems 76, 138
vanadium 65, 131
vegetables 13, 15
vitamin A 30
    A.I.D.S. 120
    cancer 93
    chronic fatigue 121
    colds and flu 119
    crohn's disease 124
    immune system 89, 94,
        121
    men 113
    menstrual problems 136,
        138
    pregnancy 107, 137
    rheumatism 129
    ulcers 127
    when to take 21
    women 111
vitamin B complex 31–7, 44,
    45, 77
    aging 105
    anxiety 132
    blood clots 123
    bowel problems 125, 127
    cancer 93
    depression 133
    energy levels 91
    headaches 134
    insomnia 103, 135
    memory 99
    men 113
    menopause 138
    premenstrual syndrome
        137
    skin problems 116, 117

stress 101
stroke 135
weight loss 97
when to take 21
women 111
vitamin B1 31
vitamin B2 32
vitamin B3 33, 123, 134
vitamin B5 34, 133, 137
vitamin B6 35
    acne 116
    asthma 118
    depression 133
    diabetes 131
    epilepsy 133
    fertility 139
    headaches 134
    heart disease 123
    immune system 89
    menstrual problems 136
vitamin B12 37, 122, 133,
    135
vitamin BC 36
vitamin C 9, 38–9
    aging 19, 94
    A.I.D.S. 120
    allergies 120
    anemia 122
    arthritis/rheumatism 128,
        129
    bowel problems 125, 138
    breathing problems 118,
        119
    cancer 93
    chronic fatigue 121
    cold sores 117
    cystitis 127
    depression 133
    diabetes 131
    fertility 136, 139
    gout 130
    heart disease 19, 123
    immune system 10, 89,
        121
    manufacture 22
    memory 99
    men 113
    menstrual problems 136,
        138
    pregnancy 137
    stress 101
    stroke 19, 135
    when to take 21
    women 111
vitamin D 42, 47
    arthritis 128
    cancer 93
    epilepsy 133
    men 113
    osteoporosis 129
    pregnancy 137
    when to take 21
    women 111
vitamin E 19, 40–1
    aging 94
    arthritis/rheumatism 128,
        129
    asthma 118
    bowel problems 125
    cancer 93
    chronic fatigue 121

diabetes 131
epilepsy 133
fertility 136, 139
heart disease 123
immune system 89, 120
men 113
menopause 138
pregnancy 137
stroke 135
when to take 21
women 111
vitamin H see biotin
vitamin K 43
vitamin P see flavonoids
vitamin Q see coenzyme Q10
vitamins 8, 14, 30–45

W

water 14
    aging 95
    bowel problems 125, 127
    colds and flu 119
    cystitis 127
    gout 130
    immune system 89
    insomnia 103
    rheumatism 129
    ulcers 127
    weight loss 97
water-soluble vitamins 14
weight loss 52, 73, 81, 84,
    96–7, 122
wholefoods 13, 15, 121, 136,
    138
withdrawal symptoms 67, 71
women 41, 110–11, 123, 127,
    136–8
wound healing 10, 34, 38, 59,
    66, 75, 78

Z

zinc 52–3
    allergies 120
    anemia 122
    arthritis/rheumatism 128,
        129
    breathing problems 118,
        119
    cancer 93
    diabetes 131
    diarrhea 127
    fertility 136, 139
    gout 130
    hyperactivity 134
    immune system 89, 121
    insomnia 103
    memory 99
    men 113
    menstrual problems 136,
        138
    pregnancy 107, 137
    premenstrual syndrome
        137
    prostate problems 139
    skin problems 116, 117
    ulcers 127
    vaginal thrush 138
    when to take 21
    women 110